ARTIST TRANSCRIPTIONS PIANO

bebop

PIANO LEGENDS

ISBN 978-1-4950-7178-2

HAL•LEONARD®

7777 W. BLUEMOUND RD. P.O. BOX 13819 MILWAUKEE, WI 53213

Visit Hal Leonard Online at
www.halleonard.com

All of You

from "Sonny Clark Trio, Vol. 3"
Words and Music by Cole Porter

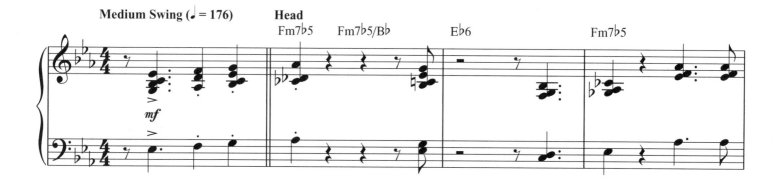

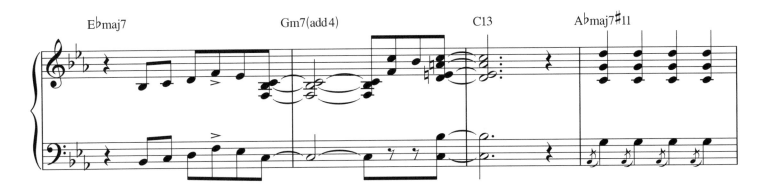

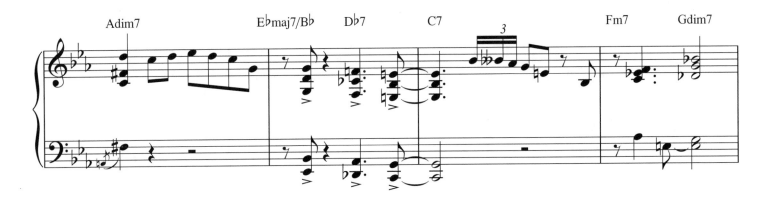

Piano Solo

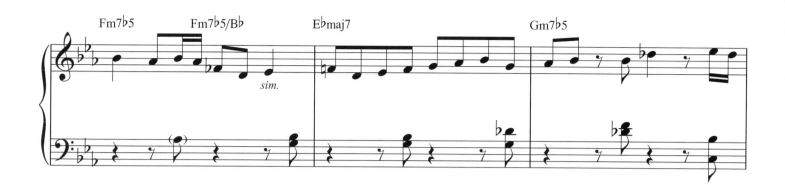

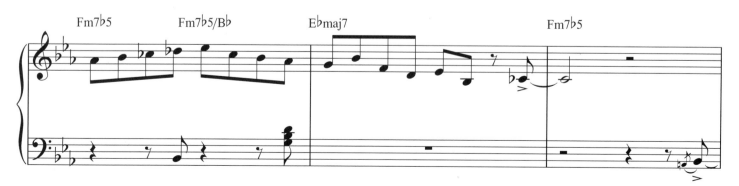

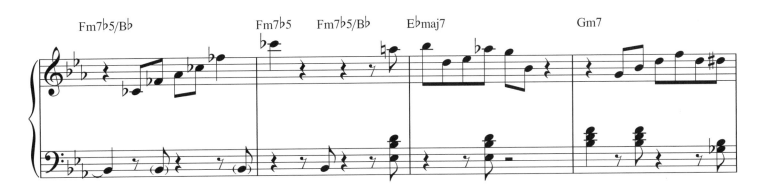

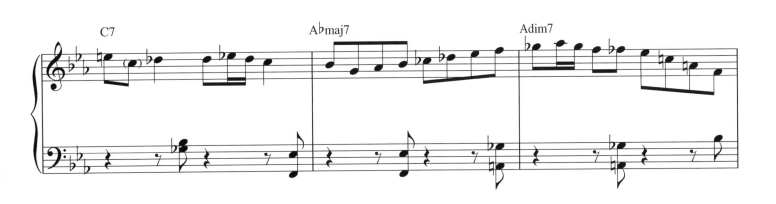

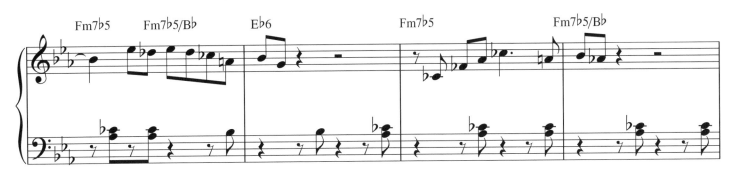

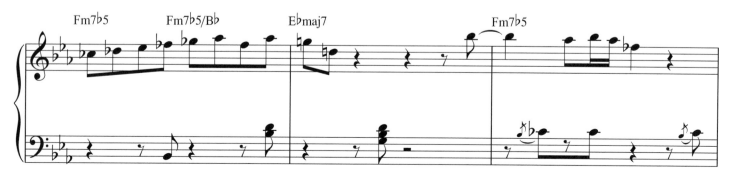

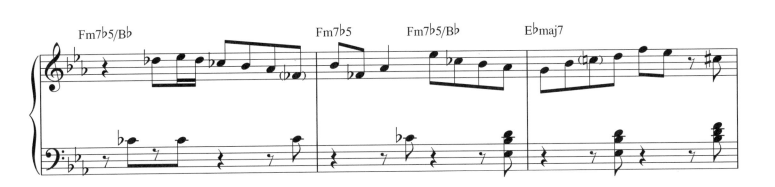

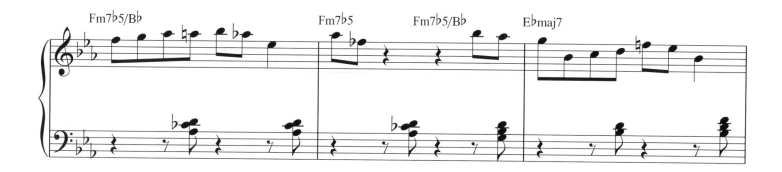

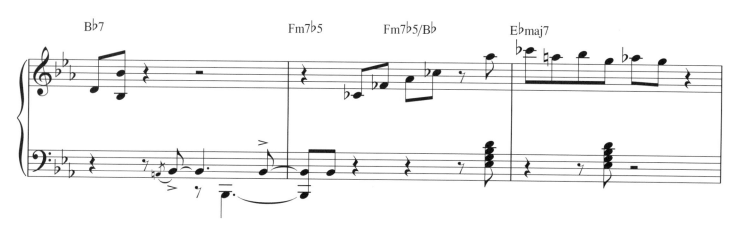

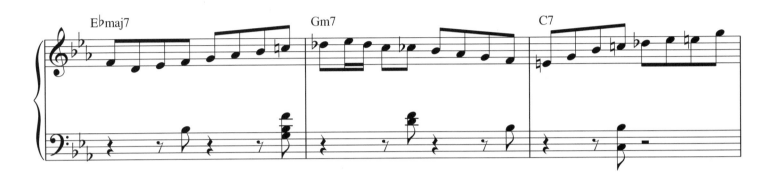

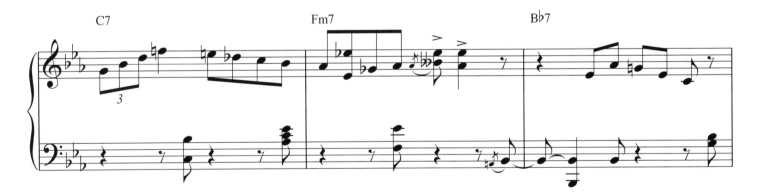

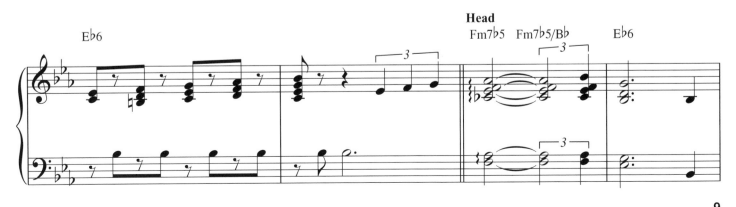

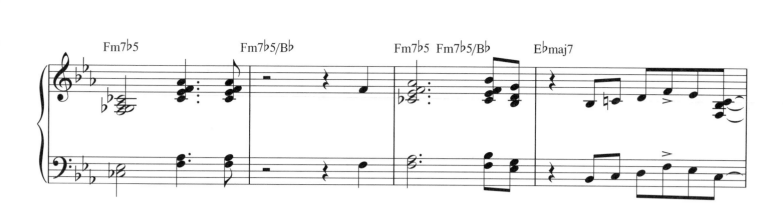

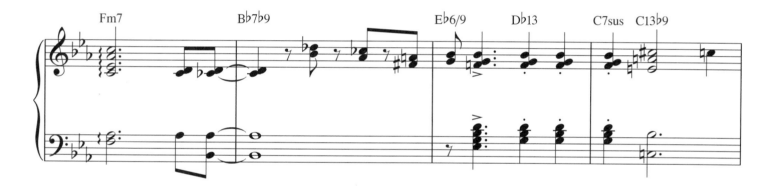

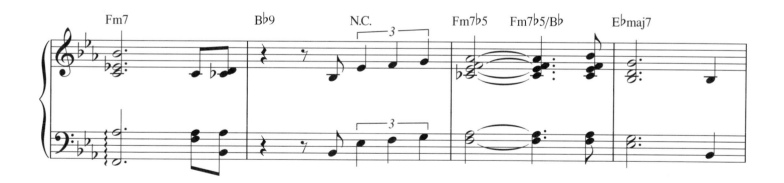

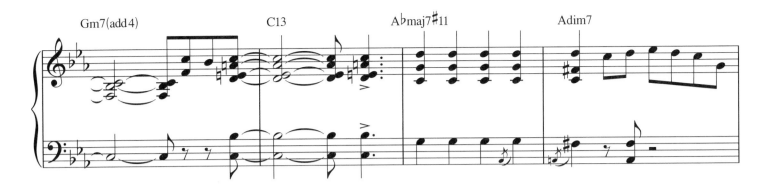

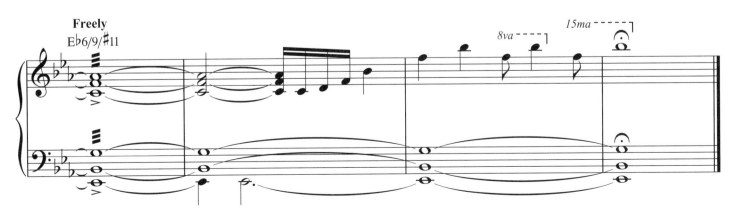

Angel Eyes
from "Ray Bryant Trio"
Words by Earl Brent
Music by Matt Dennis

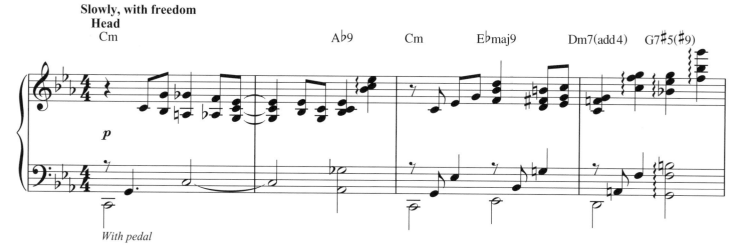

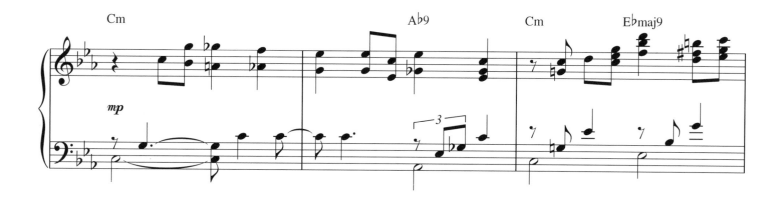

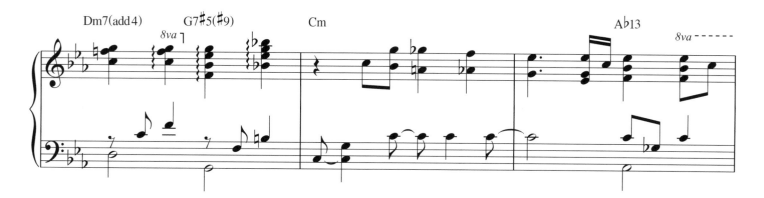

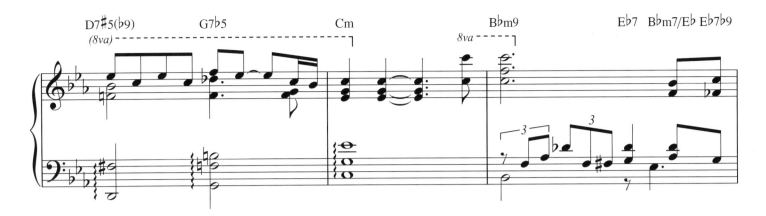

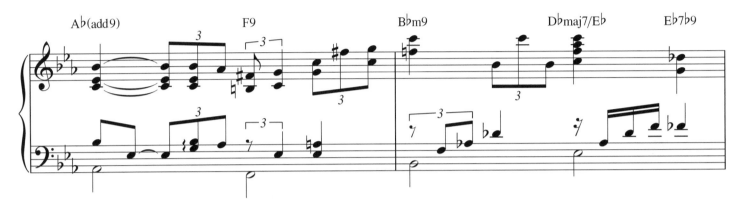

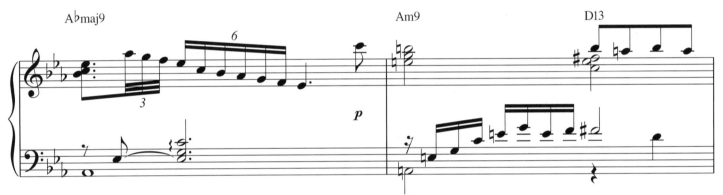

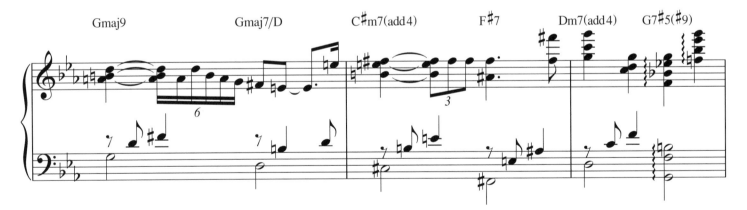

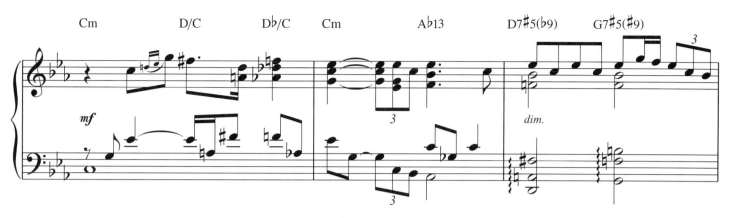

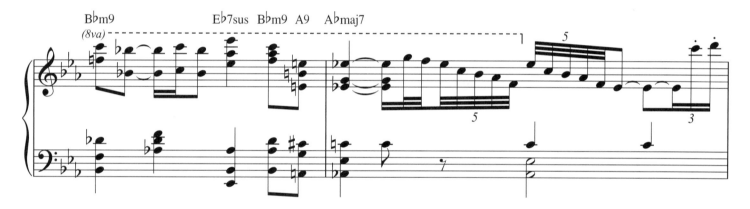

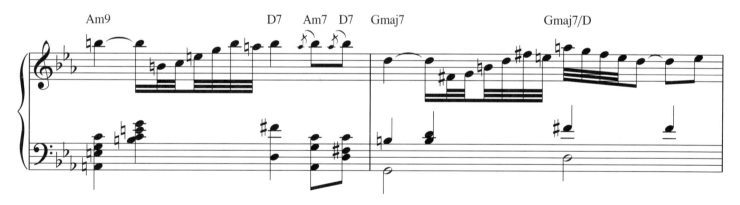

Autumn Leaves

from McCoy Tyner "Today and Tomorrow"
English lyric by Johnny Mercer
French lyric by Jacques Prevert
Music by Joseph Kosma

Head

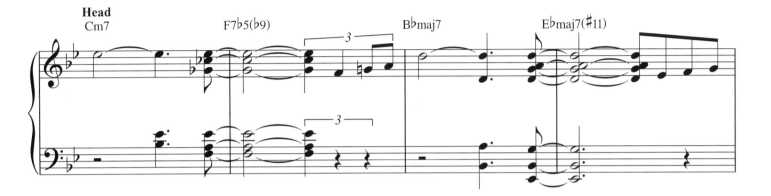

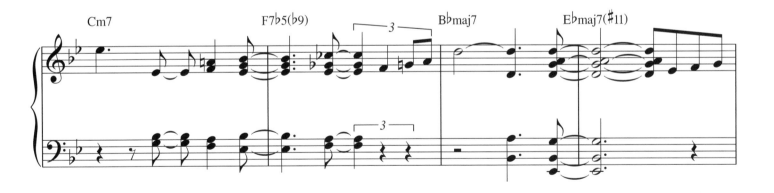

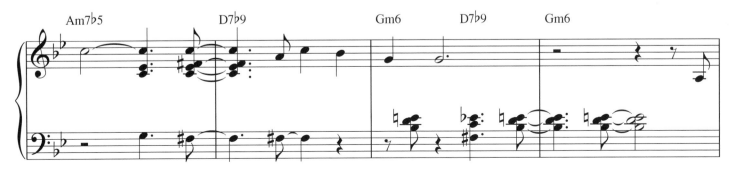

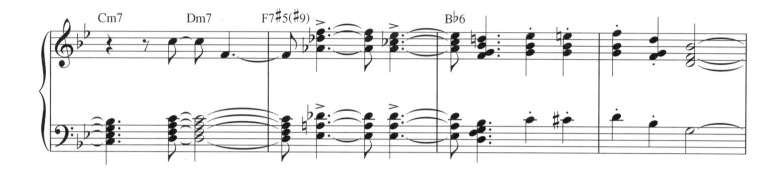

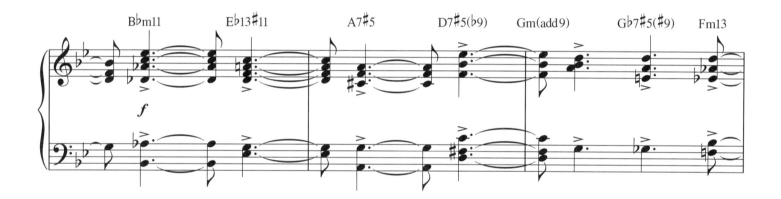

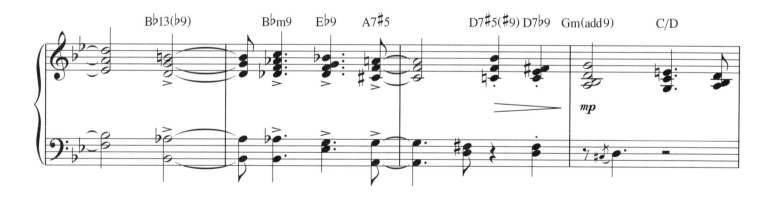

Piano Solo

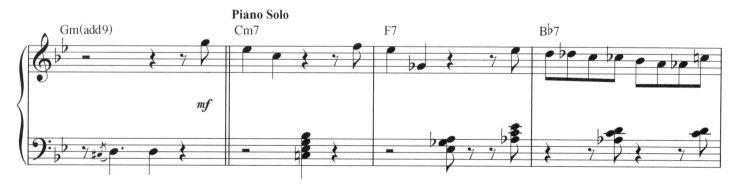

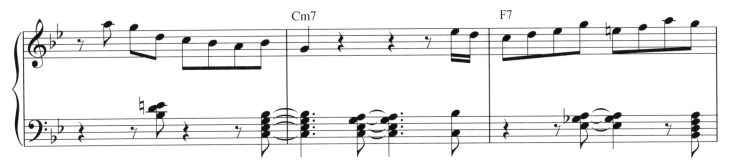

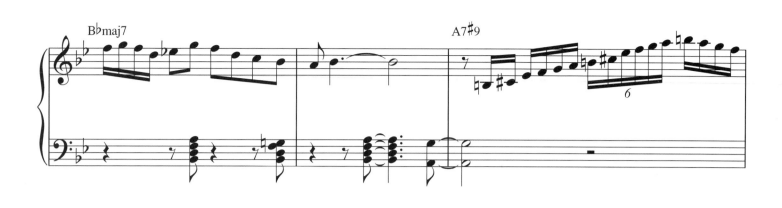

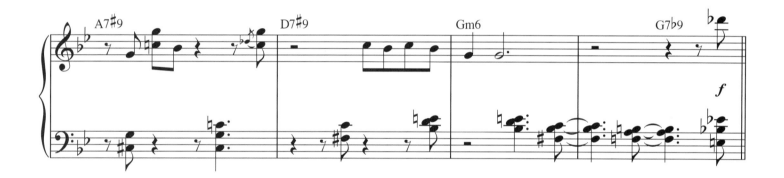

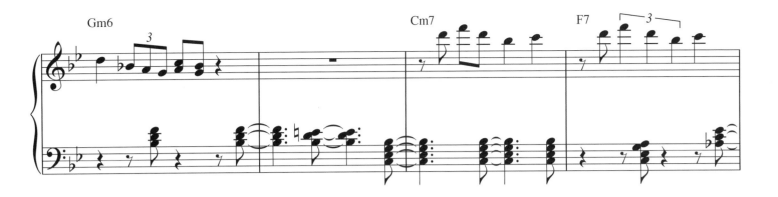

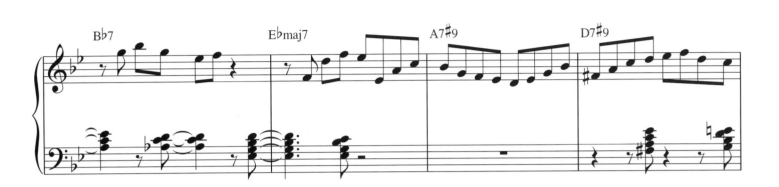

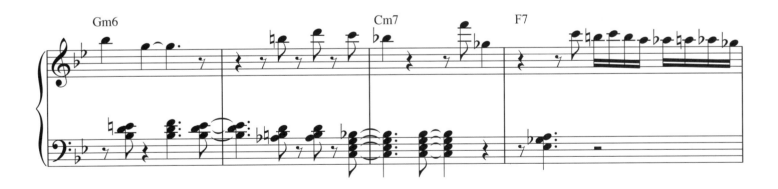

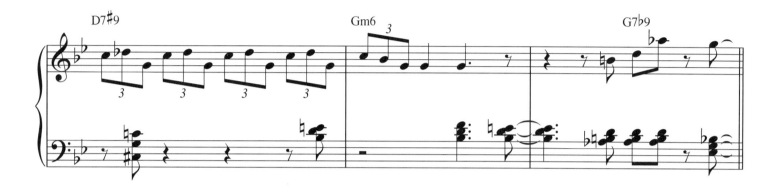

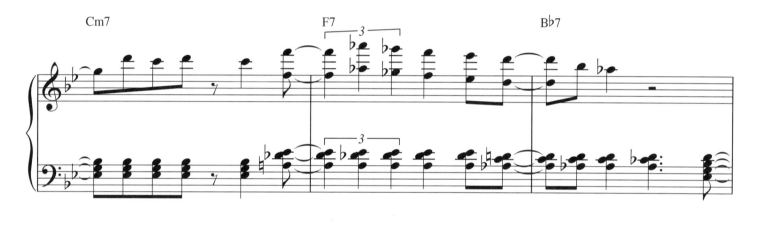

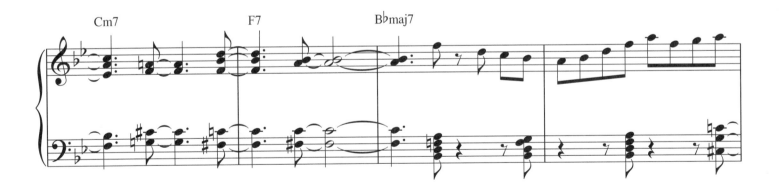

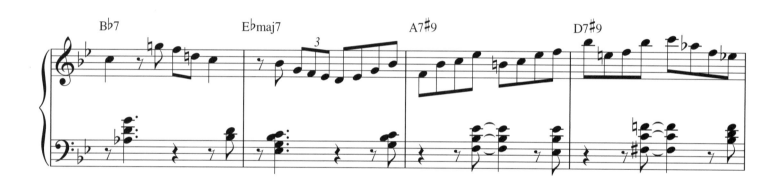

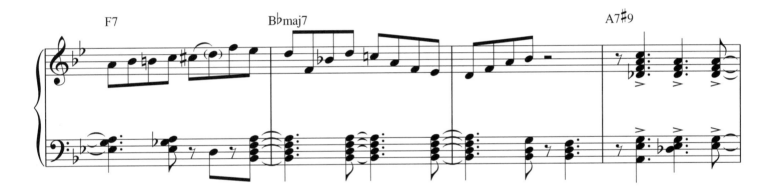

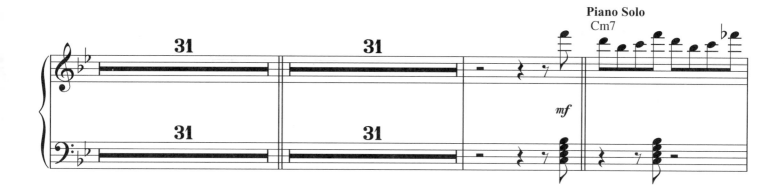

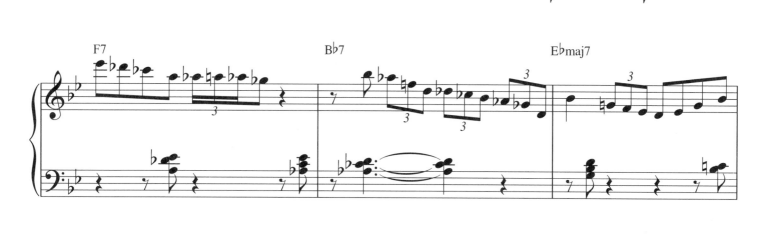

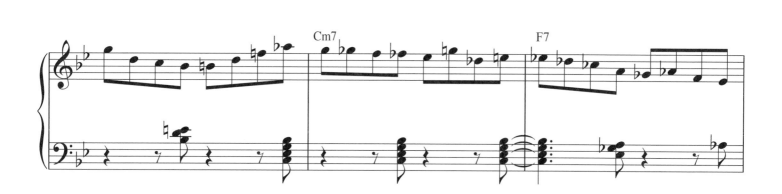

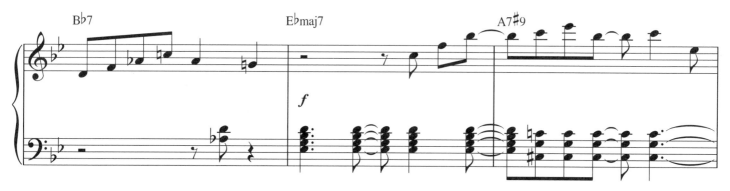

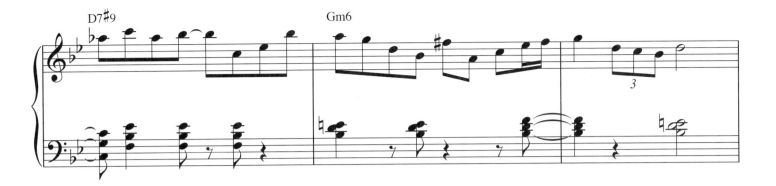

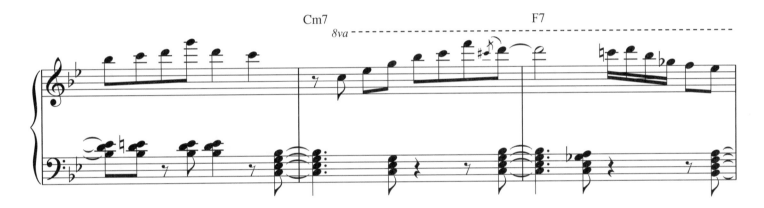

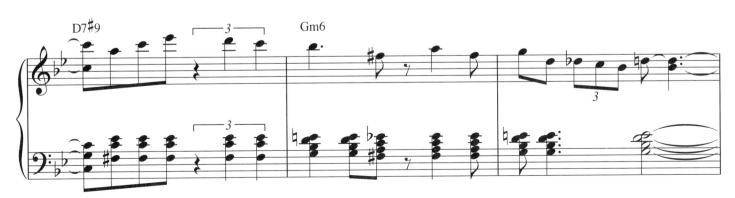

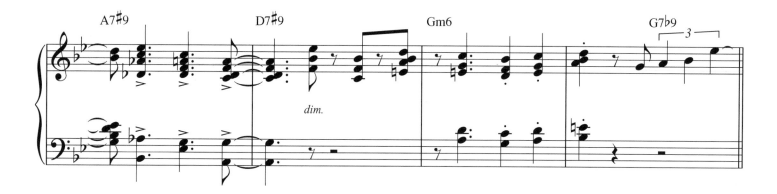

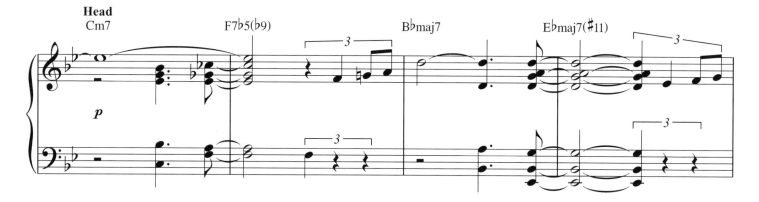

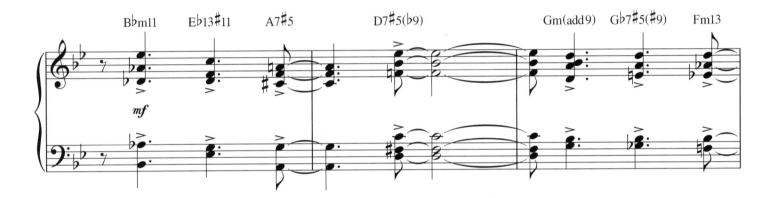

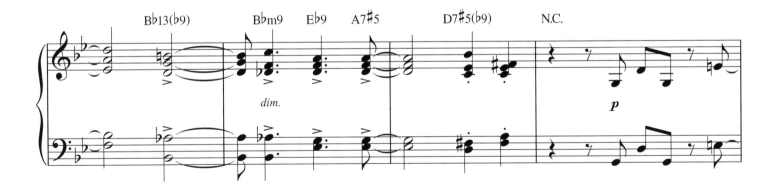

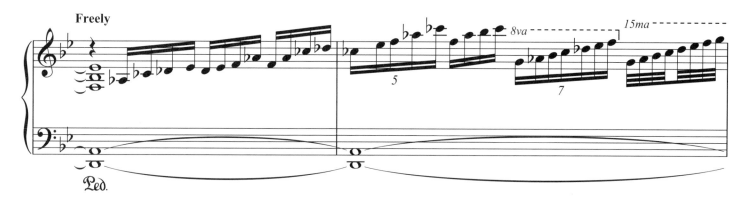

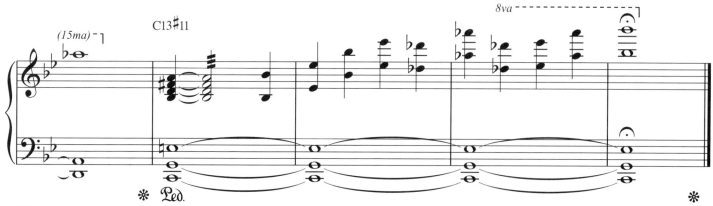

Cheryl

from Phineas Newborn Jr. "A World of Piano!"

By Charlie Parker

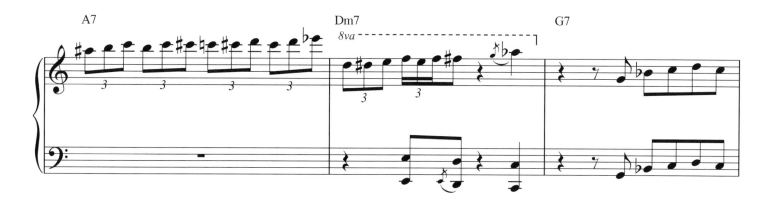

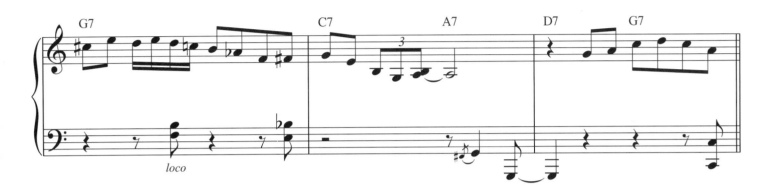

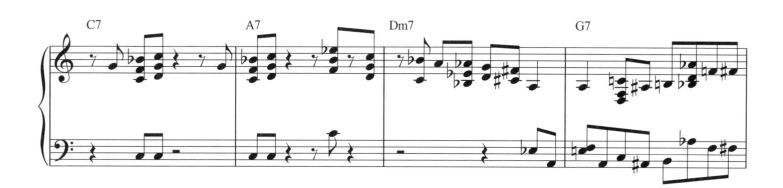

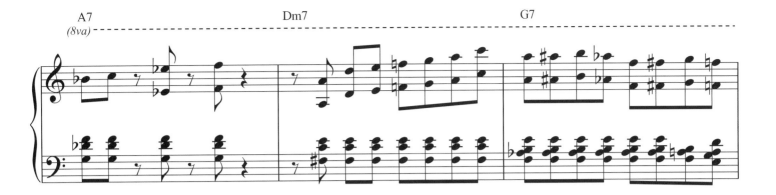

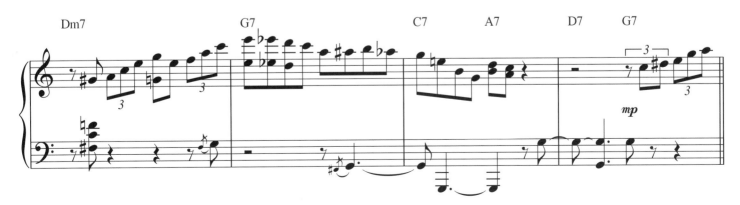

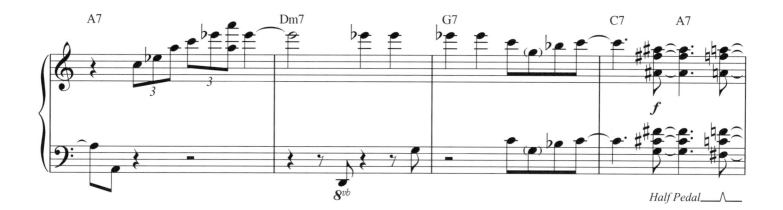

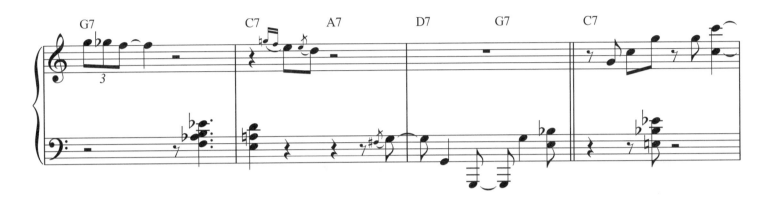

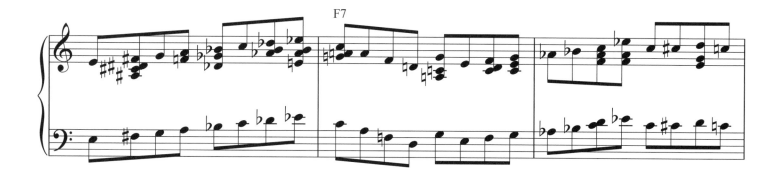

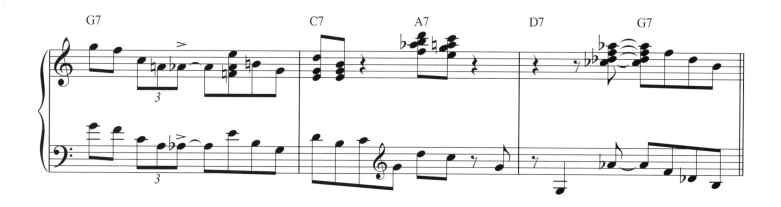

Head

A Foggy Day

(In London Town)
from "Red Garland Trio - A Garland of Red"
Music and Lyrics by George Gershwin and Ira Gershwin

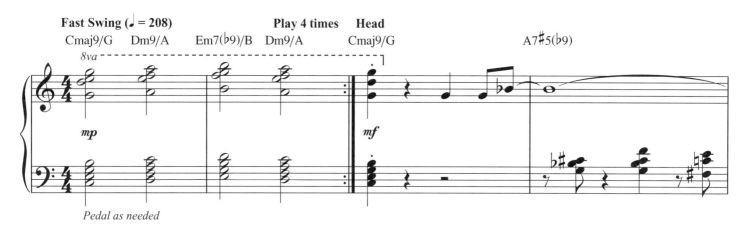

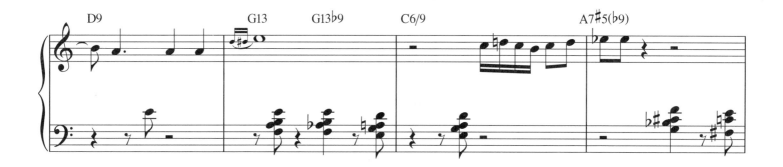

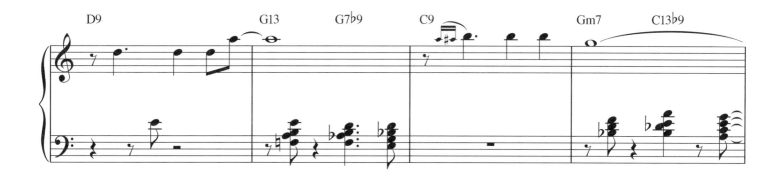

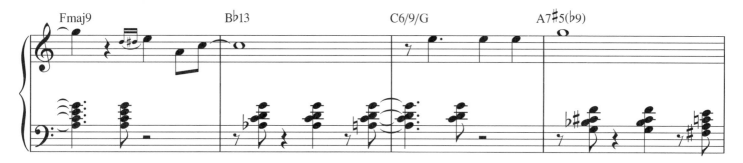

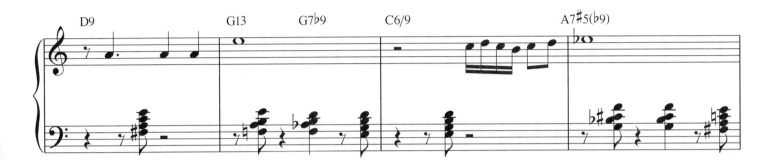

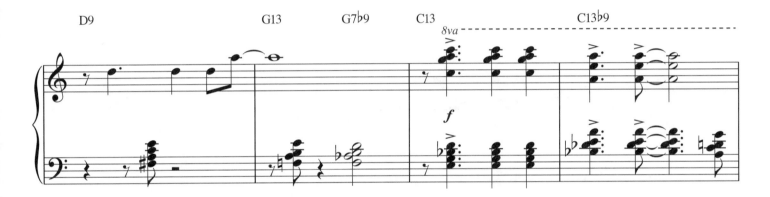

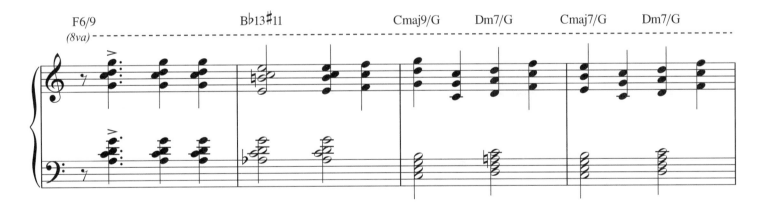

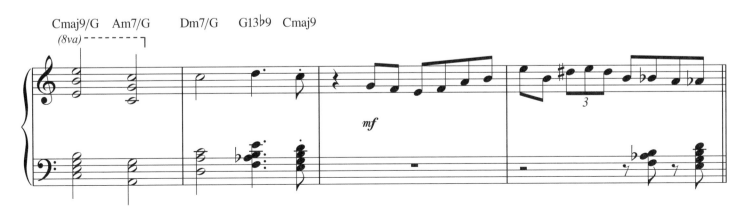

Piano Solo

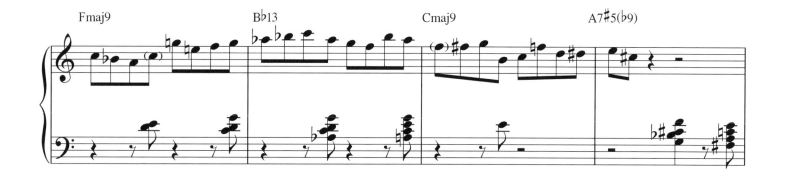

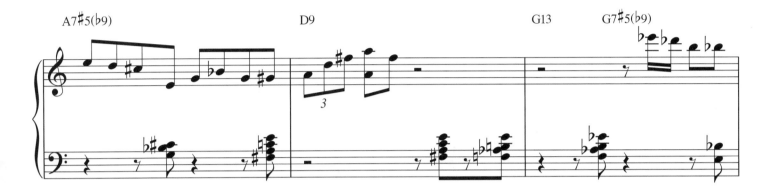

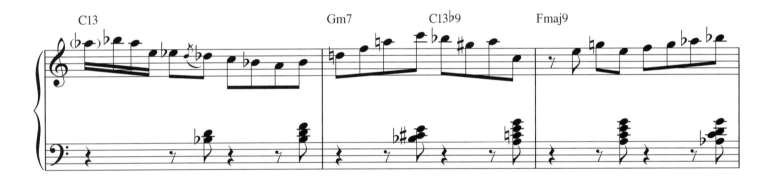

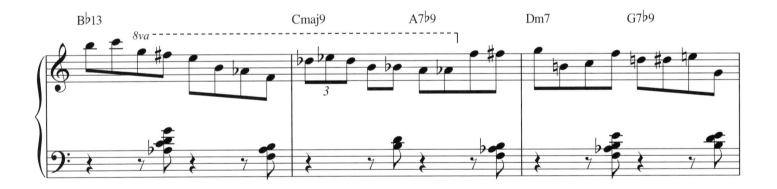

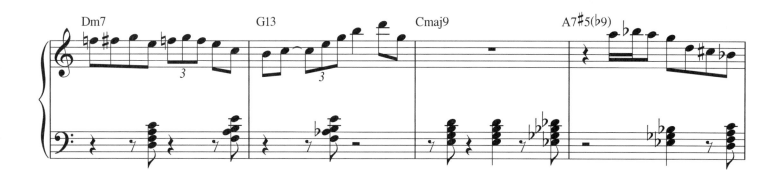

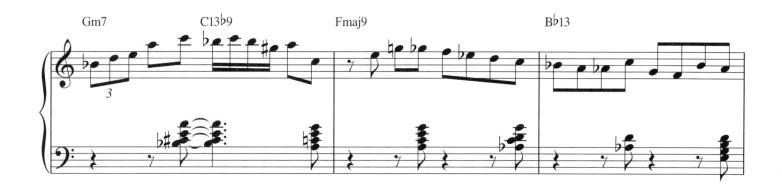

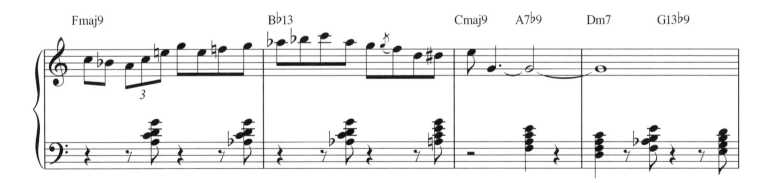

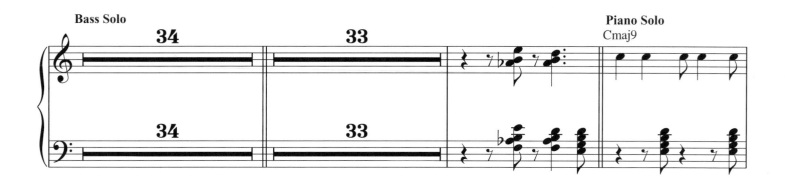

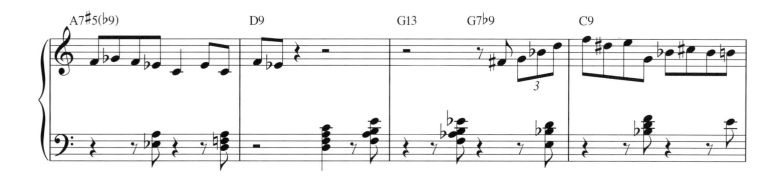

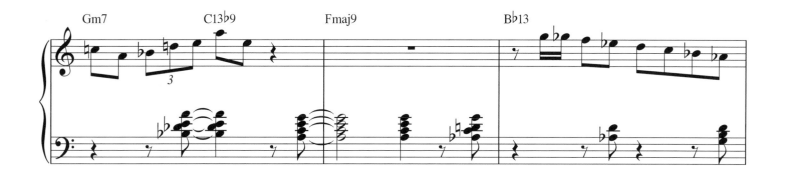

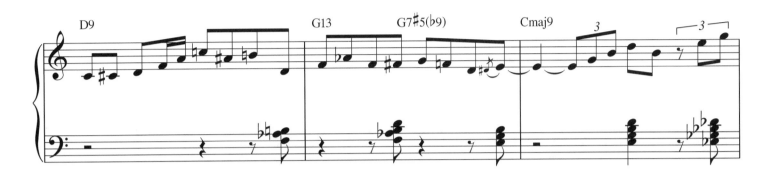

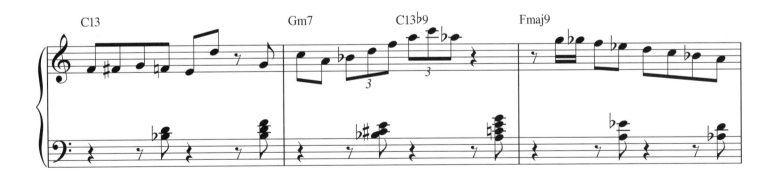

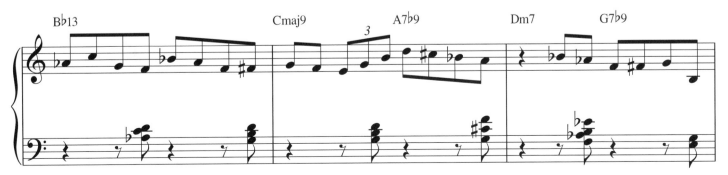

Head

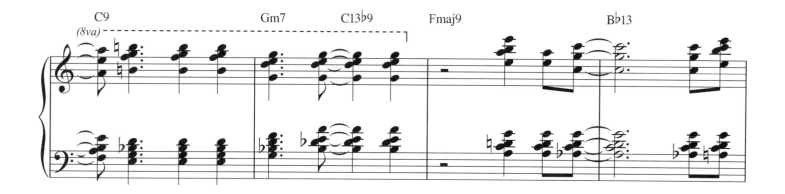

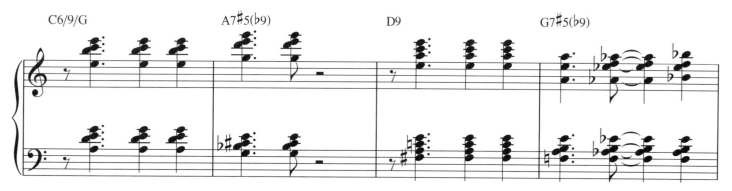

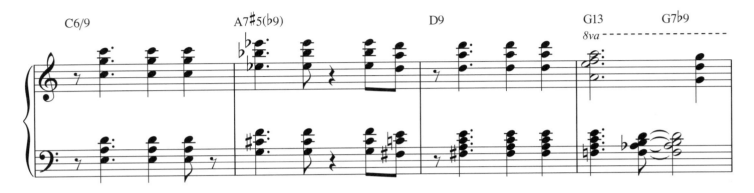

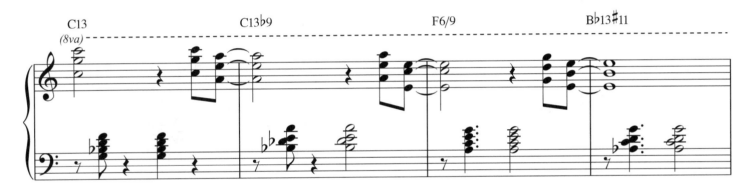

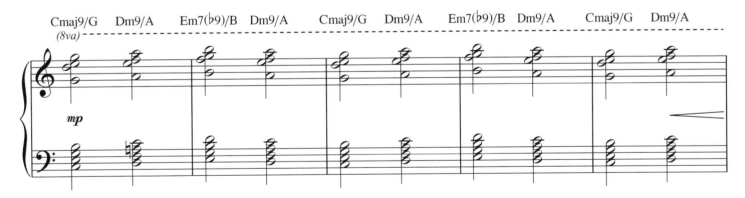

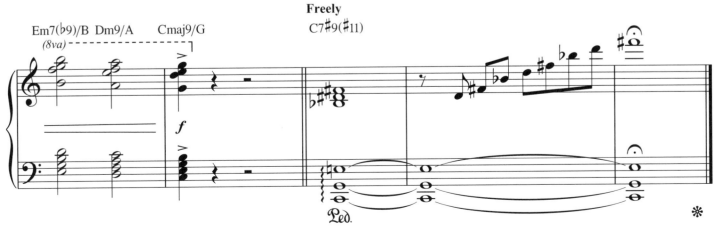

Golden Earrings

from "The Ray Bryant Trio"

Words by Jay Livingston and Ray Evans
Music by Victor Young

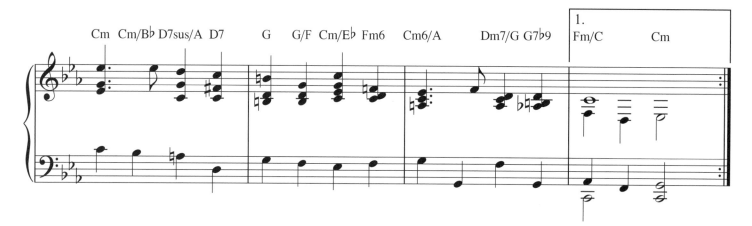

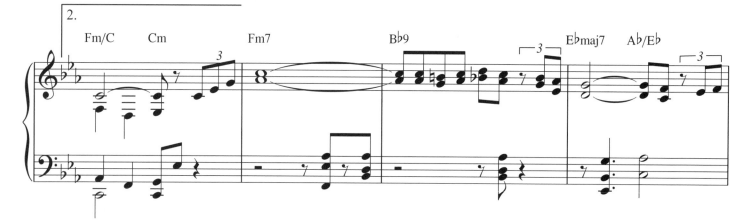

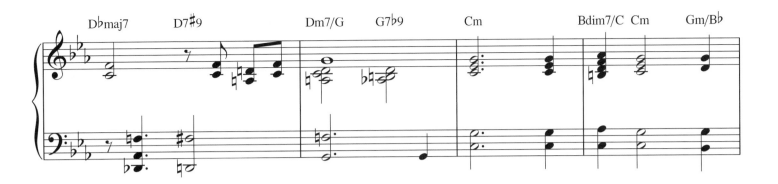

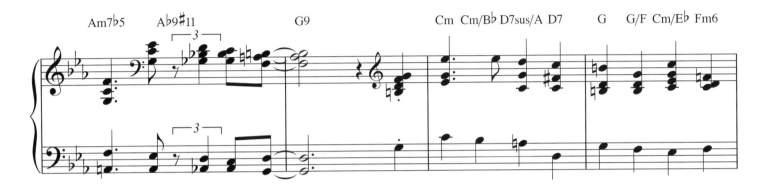

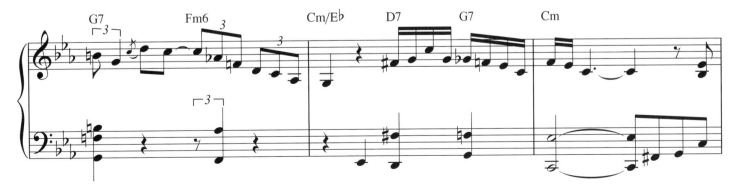

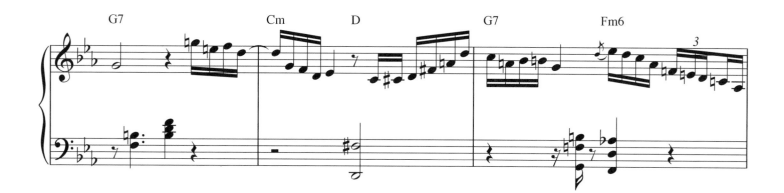

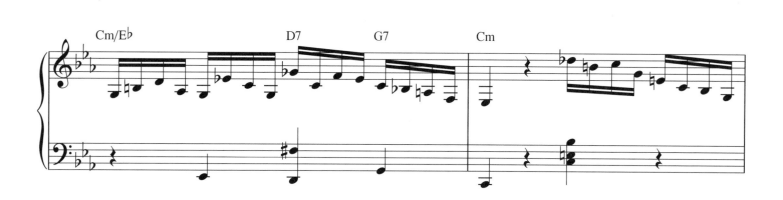

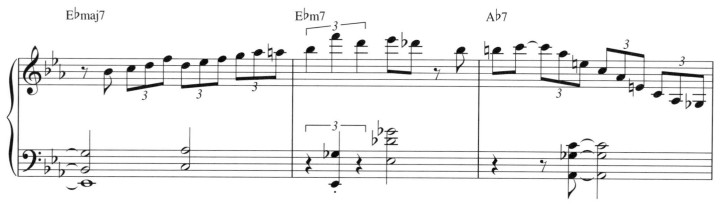

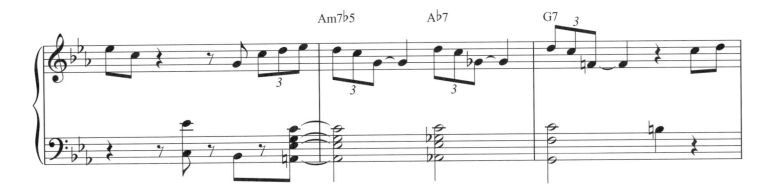

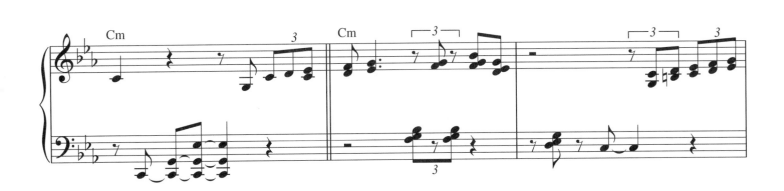

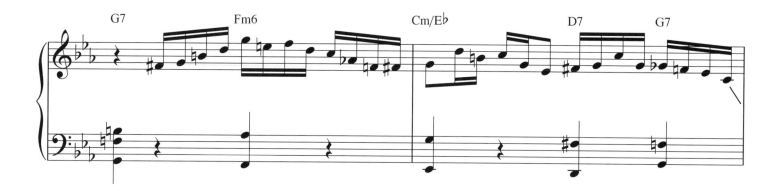

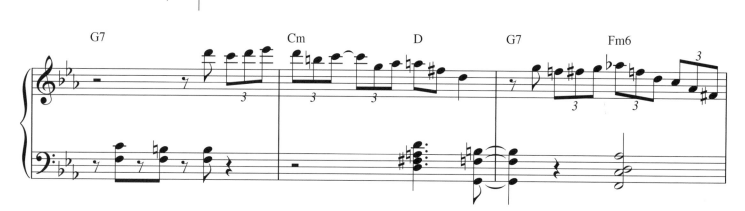

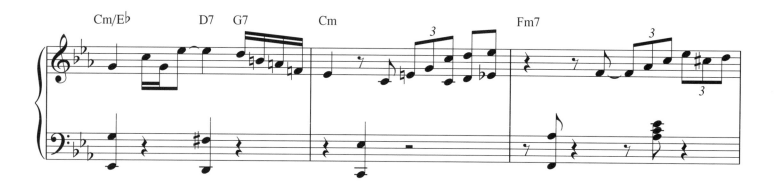

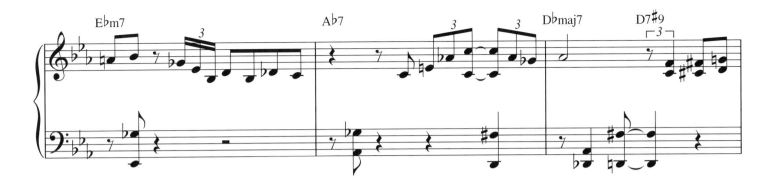

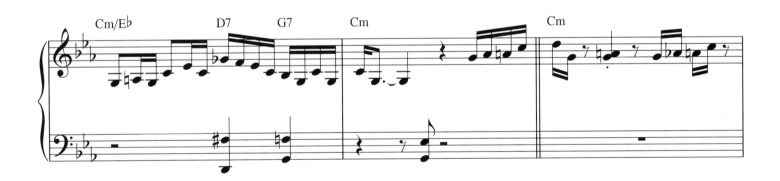

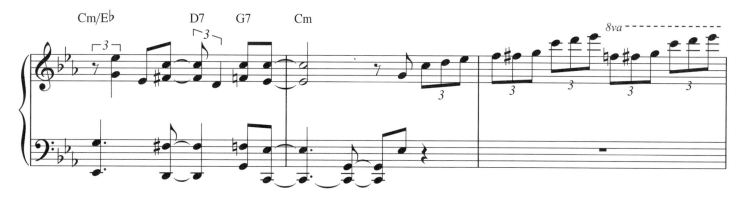

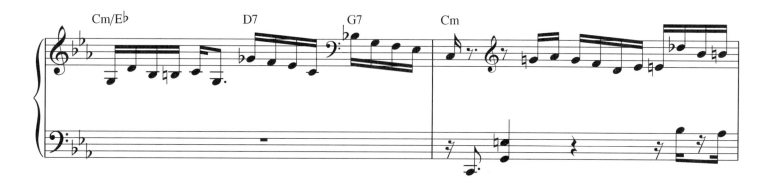

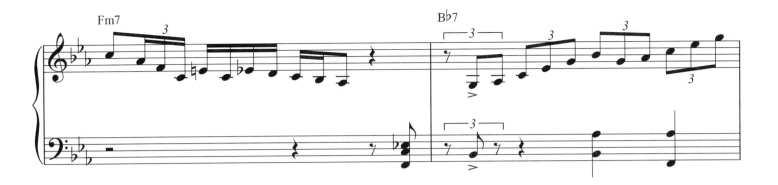

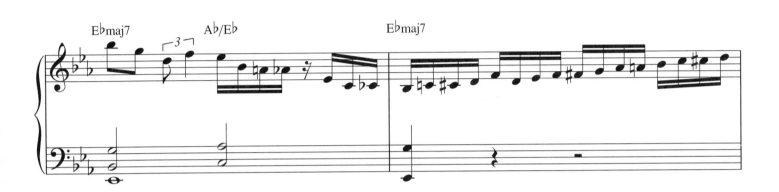

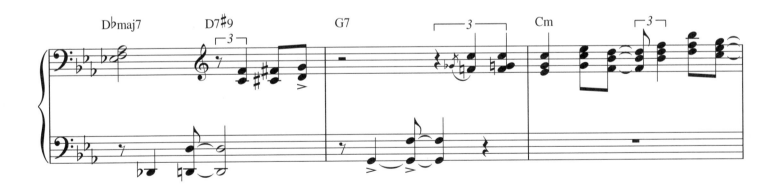

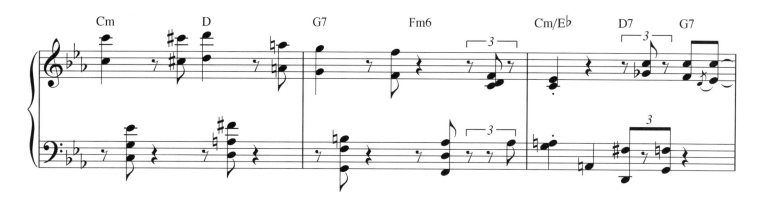

Head

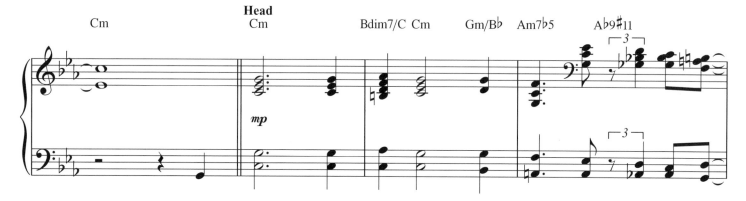

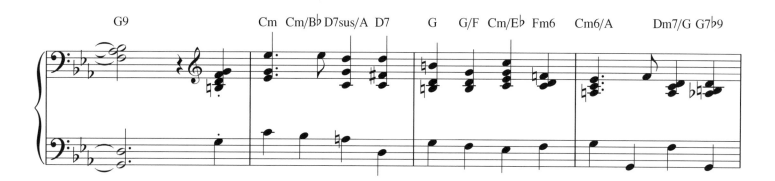

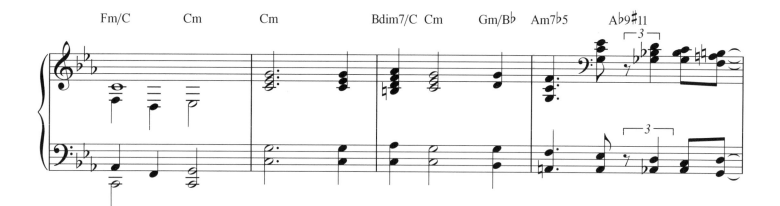

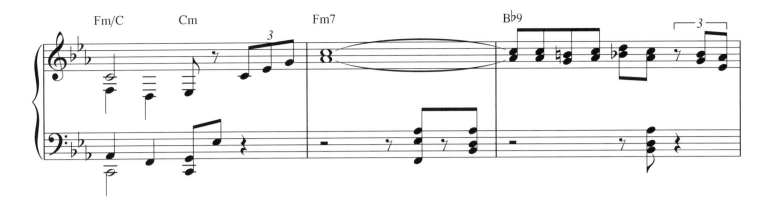

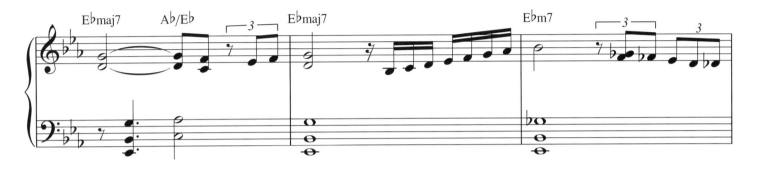

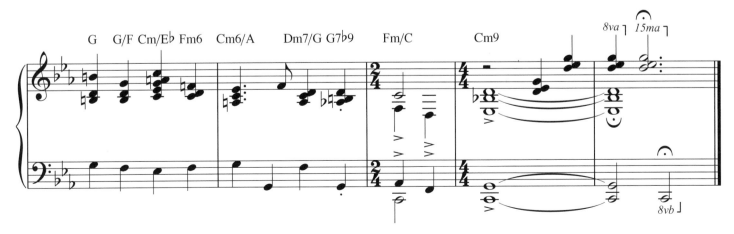

Groovin' High
from Bobby Timmons "Easy Does It"
By John "Dizzy" Gillespie

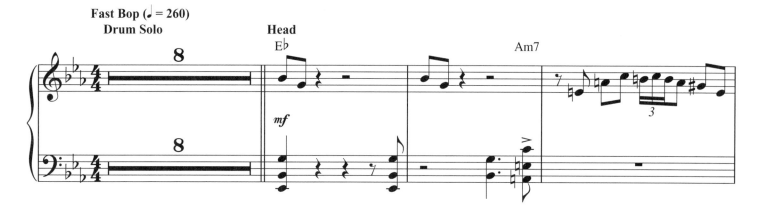

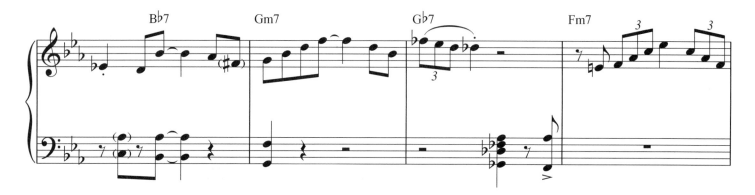

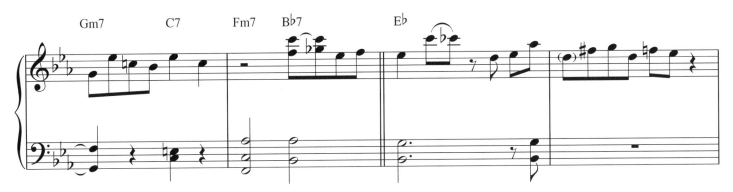

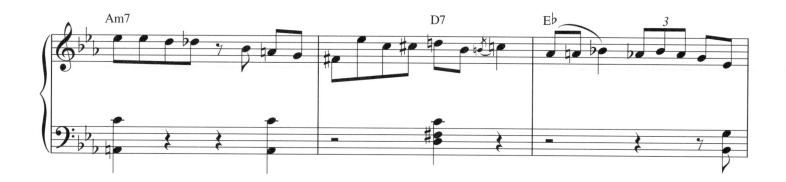

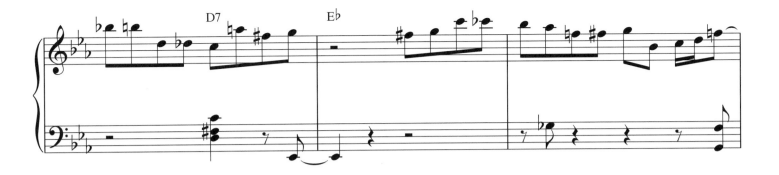

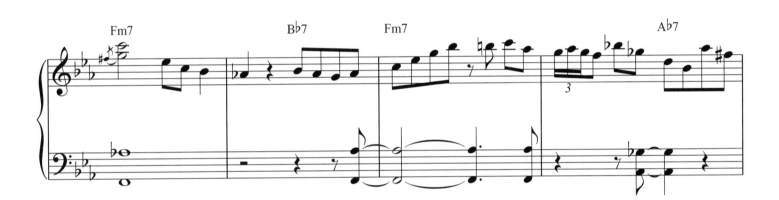

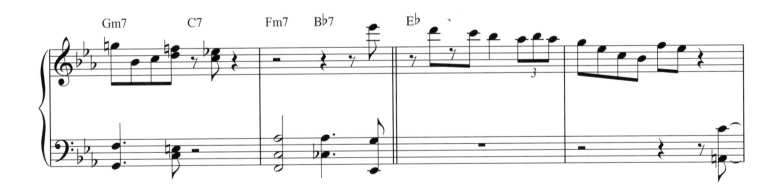

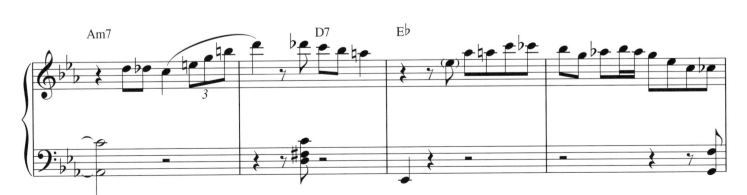

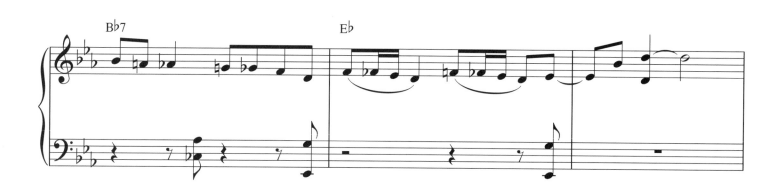

Piano Trades 4's with Drums

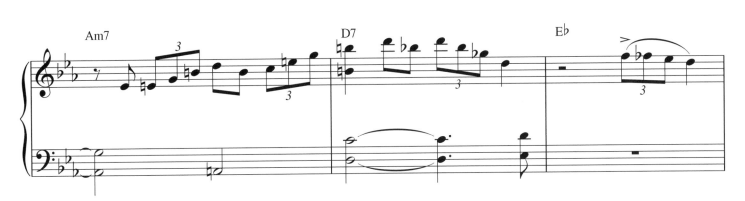

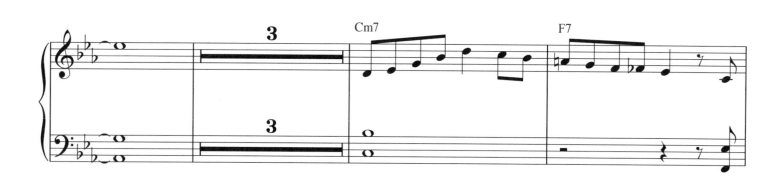

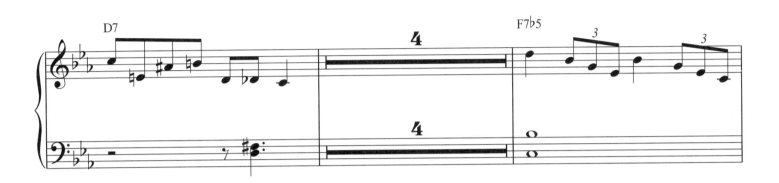

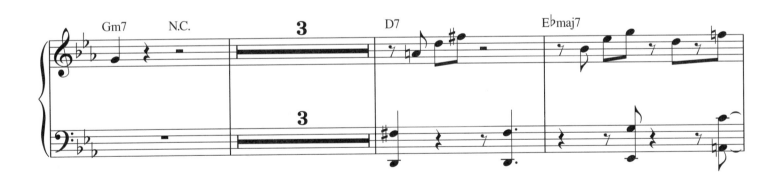

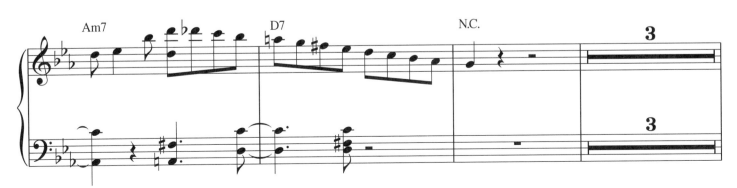

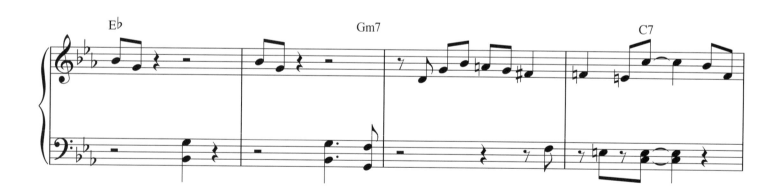

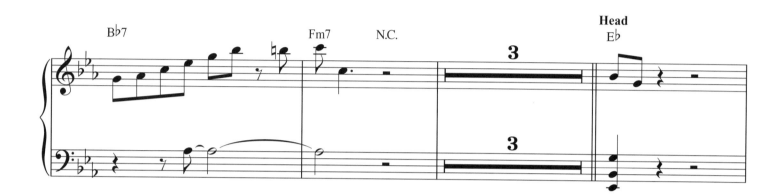

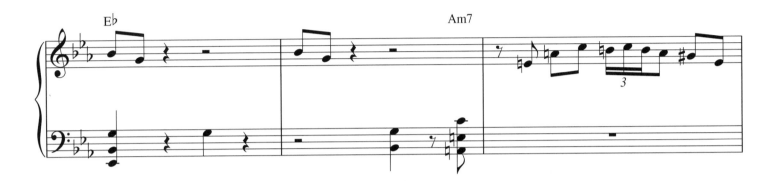

It's a Lovely Day Today

from Elmo Hope "Trio and Quintet"
Words and Music by Irving Berlin

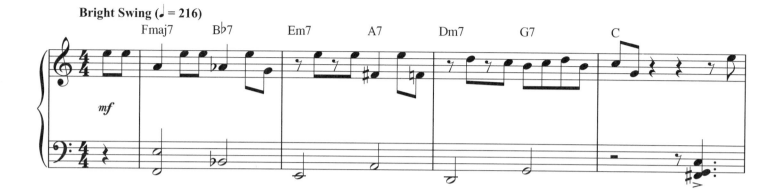

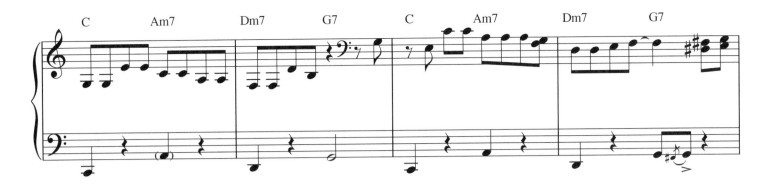

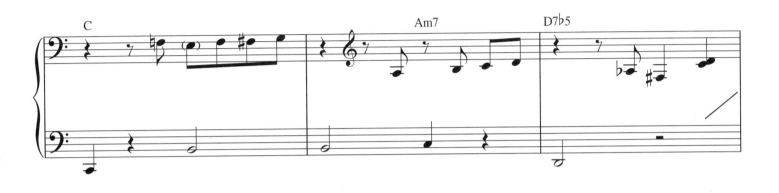

Piano Solo

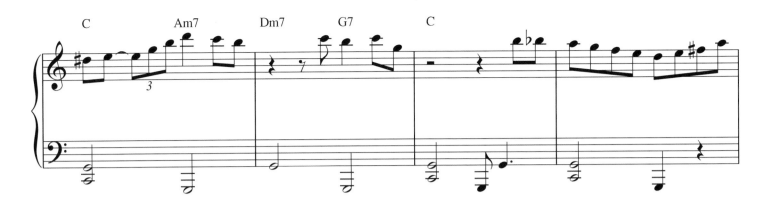

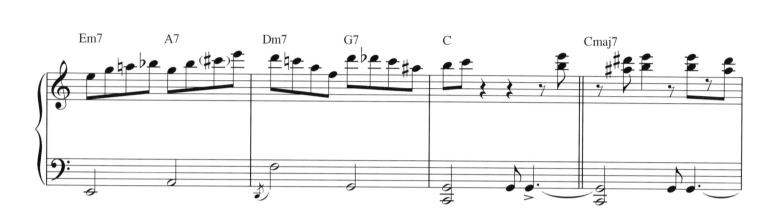

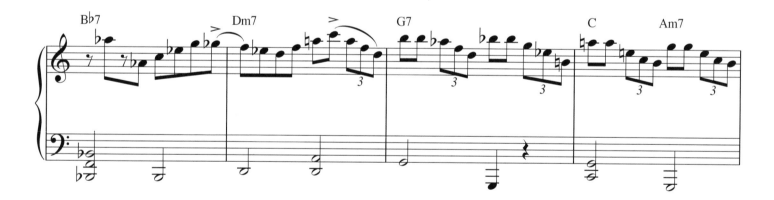

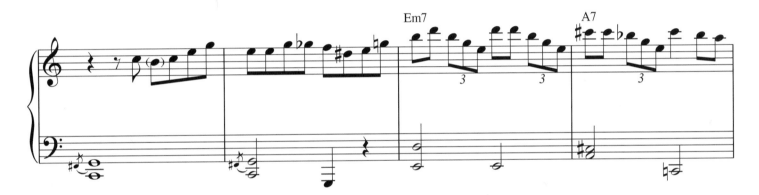

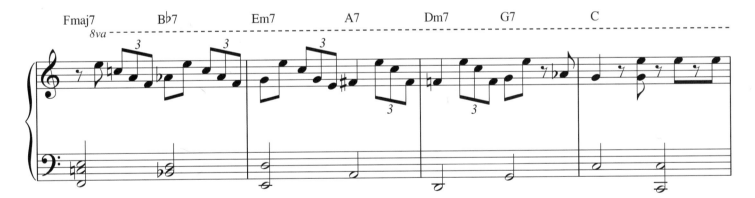

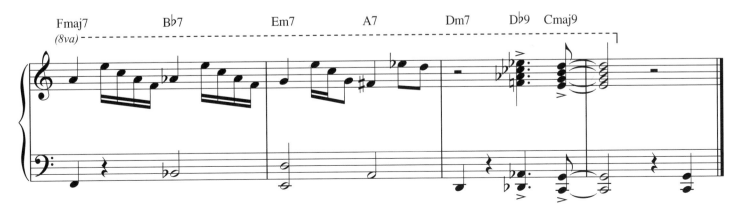

Just One of Those Things
from Hampton Hawes "Trio and Quartet 1951-1956"
Words and Music by Cole Porter

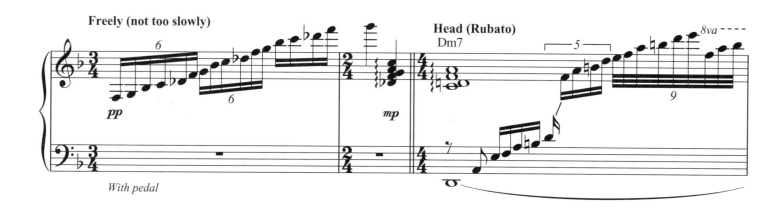

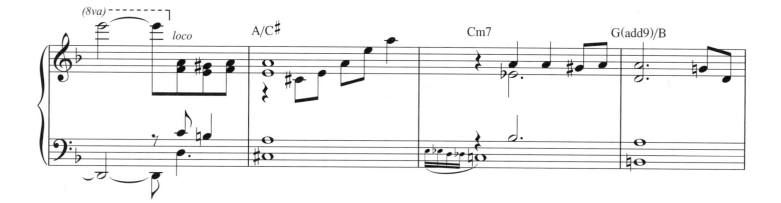

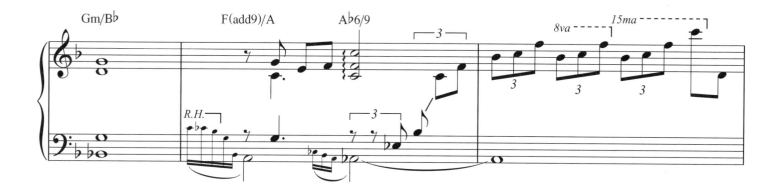

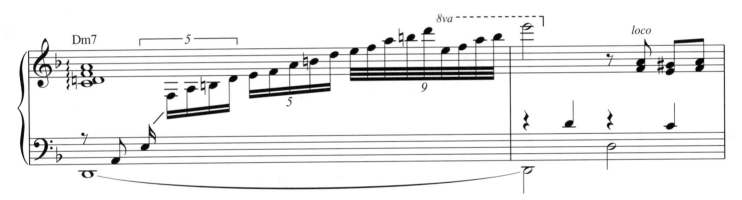

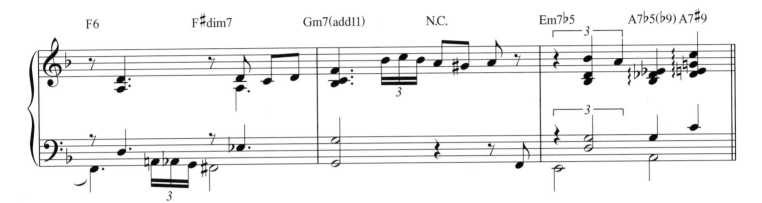

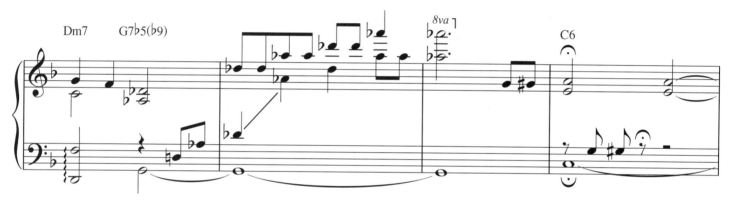

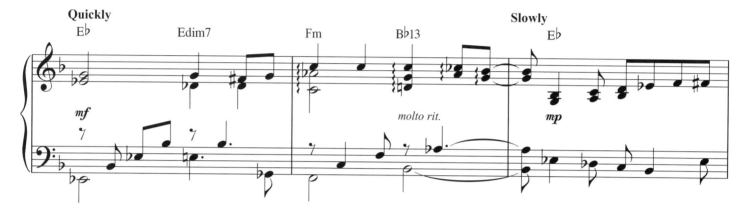

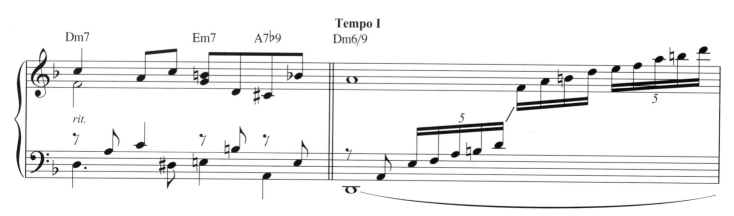

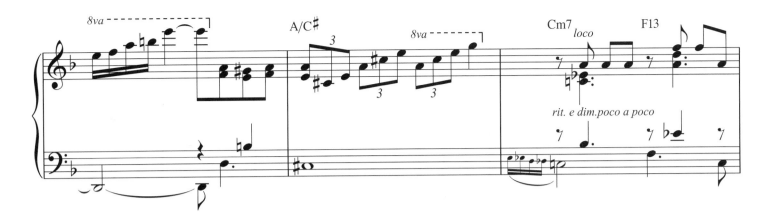

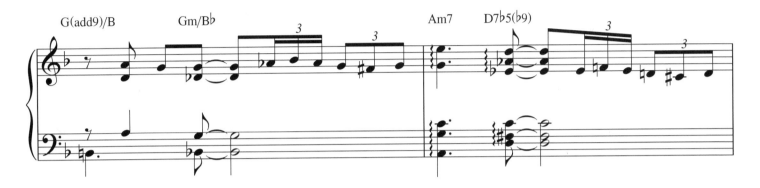

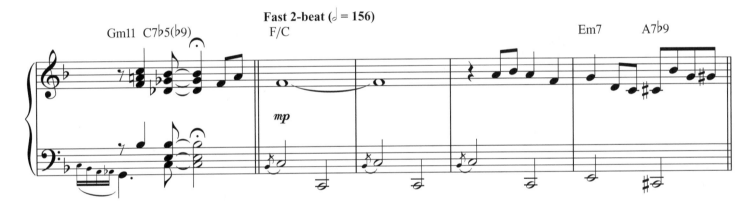

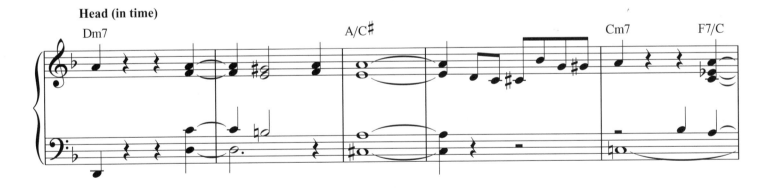

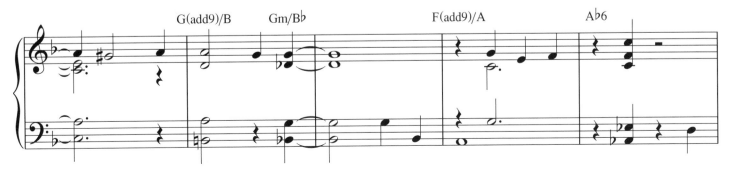

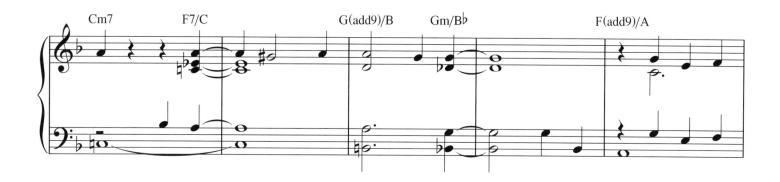

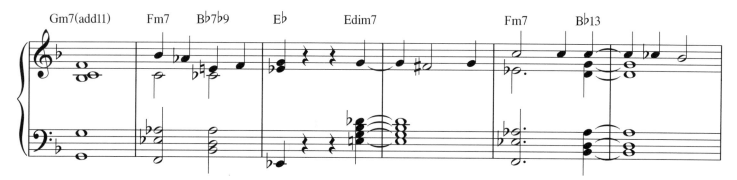

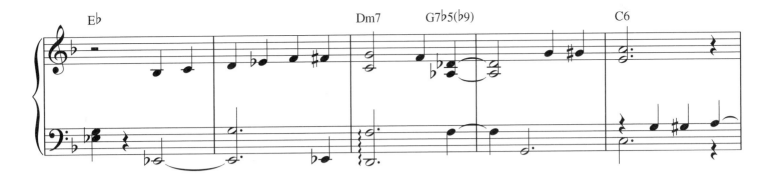

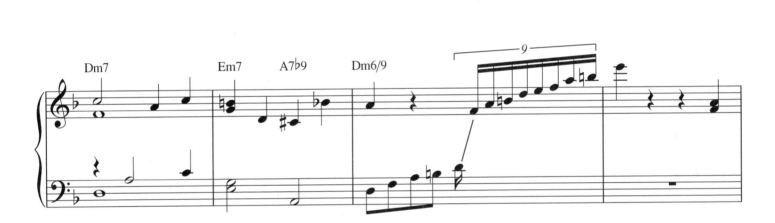

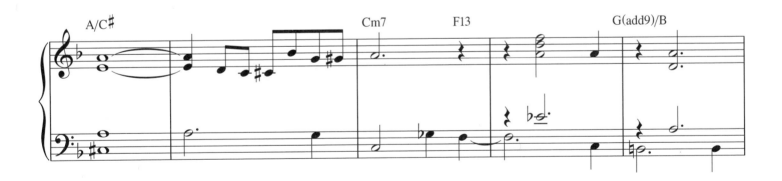

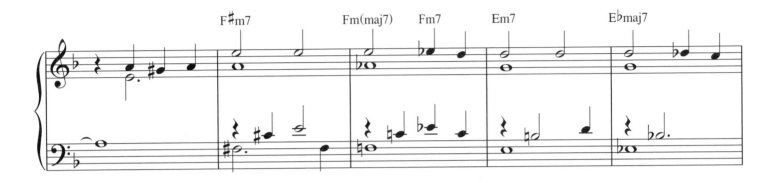

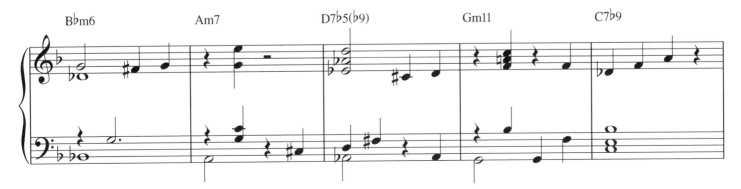

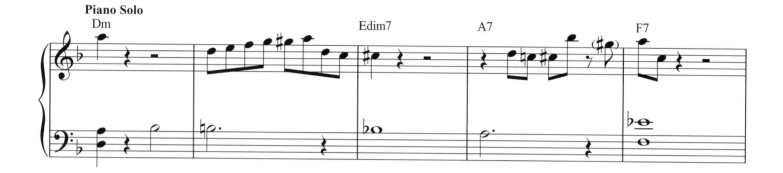

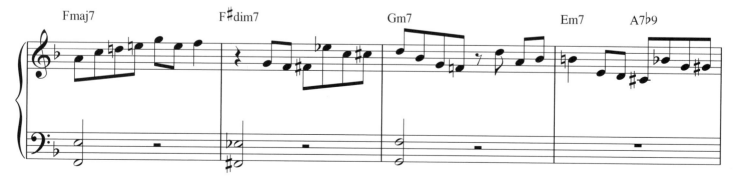

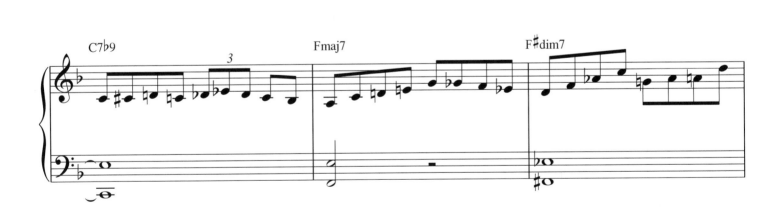

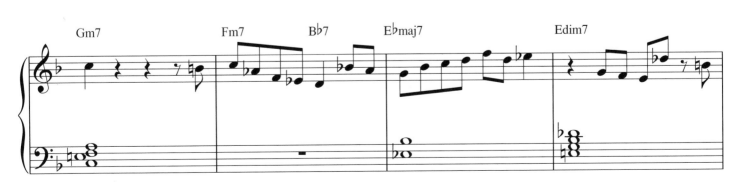

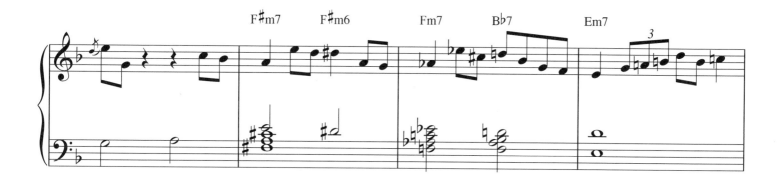

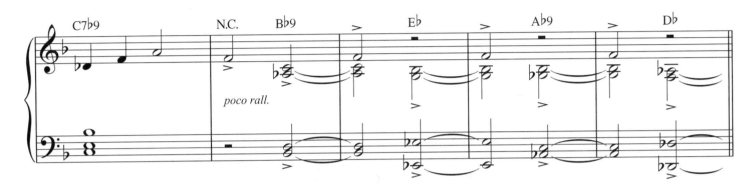

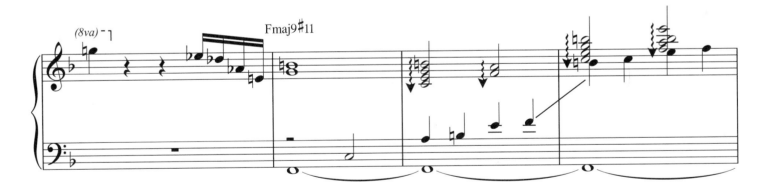

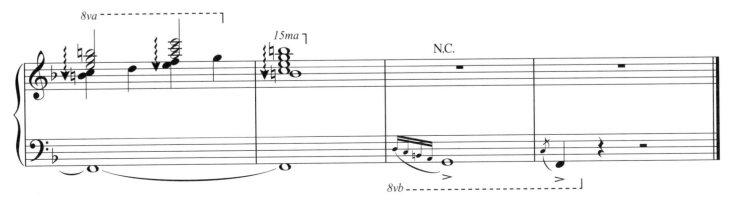

Lullaby of Birdland

from Jaki Byard "Hi-Fly"
Words by George David Weiss
Music by George Shearing

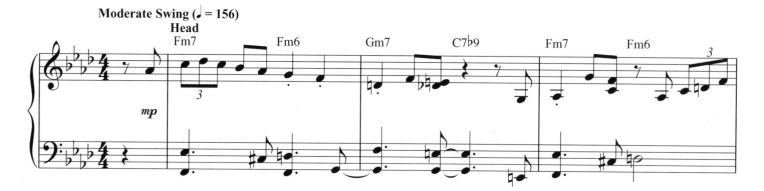

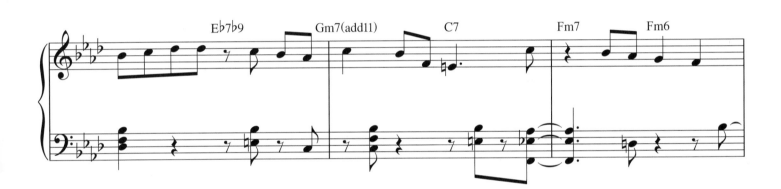

Piano Solo

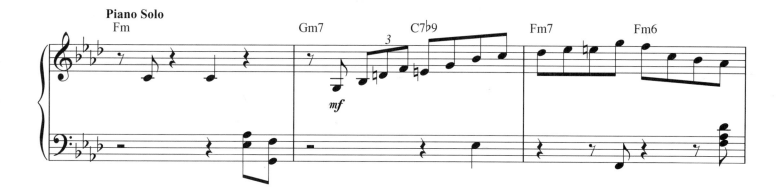

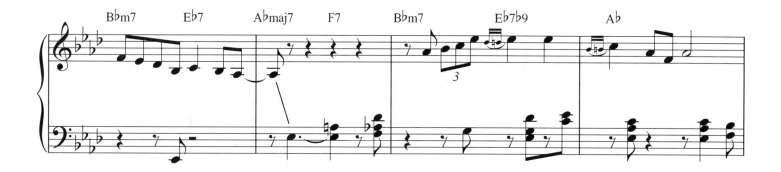

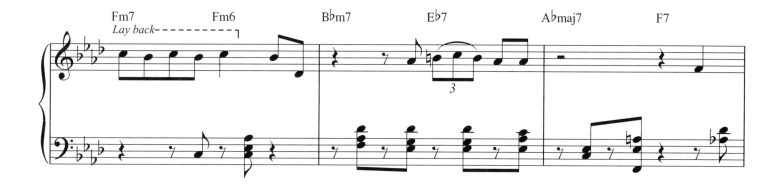

94

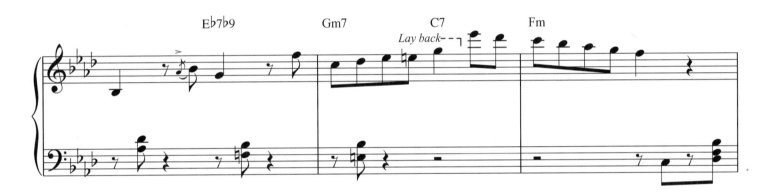

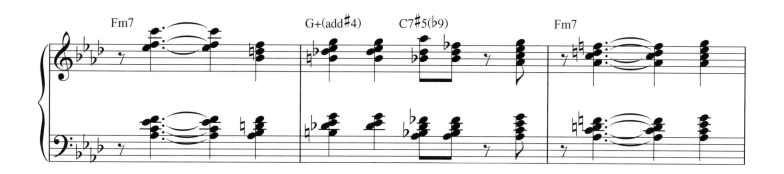

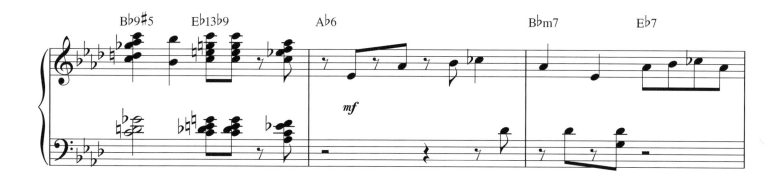

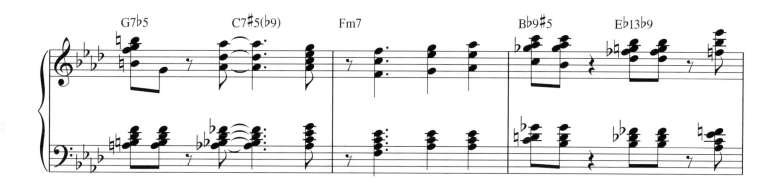

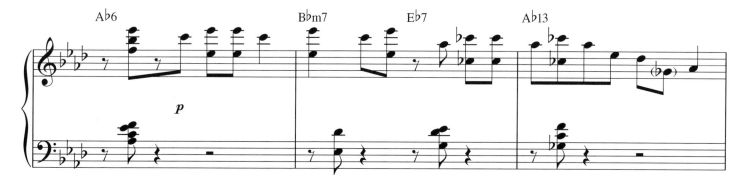

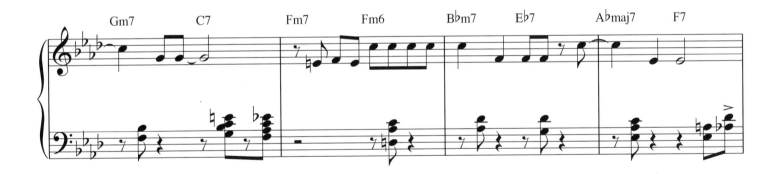

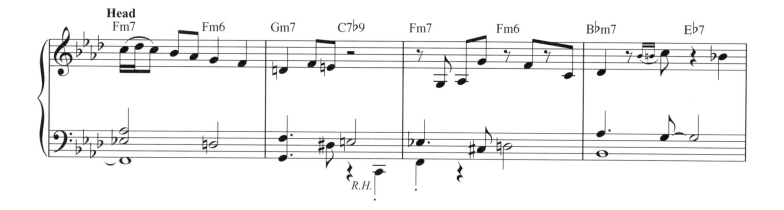

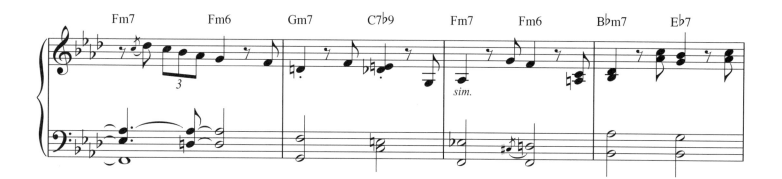

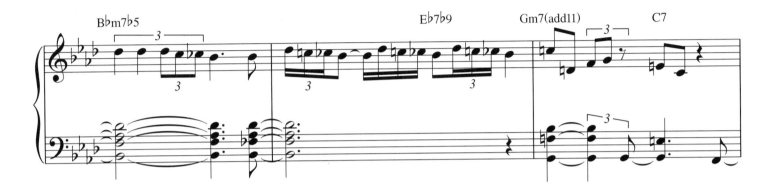

Sweet and Lovely

from "Thelonious Monk Trio"

Words and Music by Gus Arnheim, Charles N. Daniels and Harry Tobias

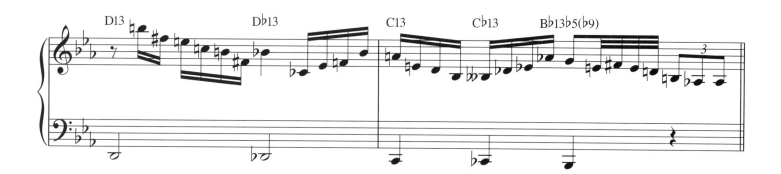

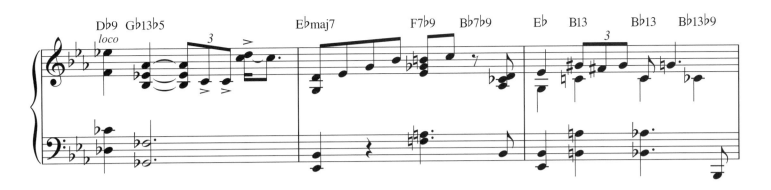

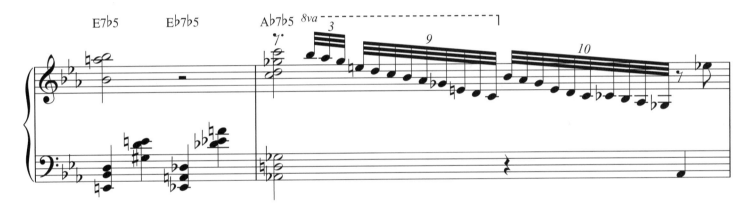

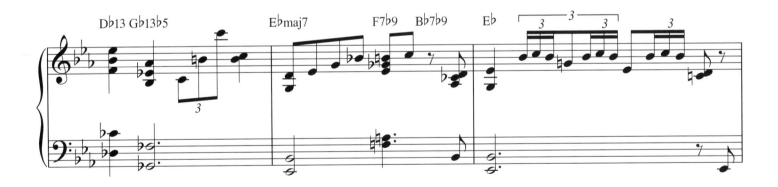

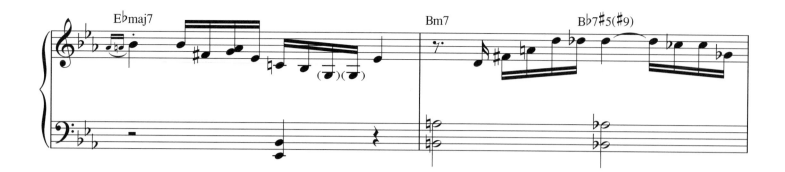

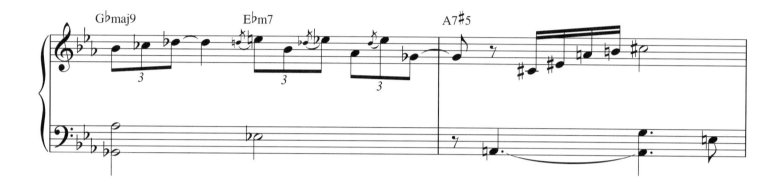

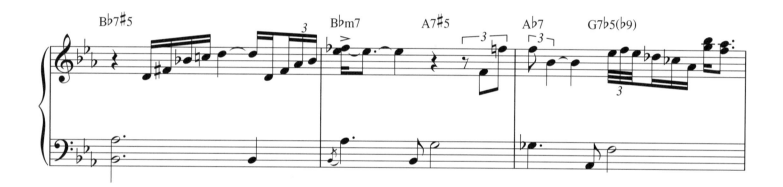

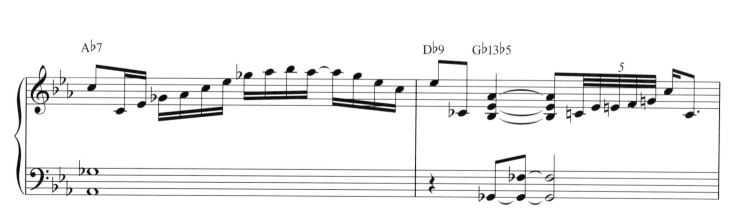

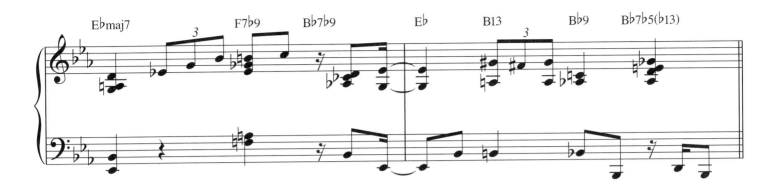

Double Time
Piano Solo

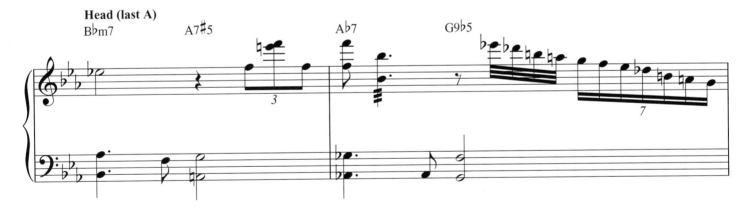

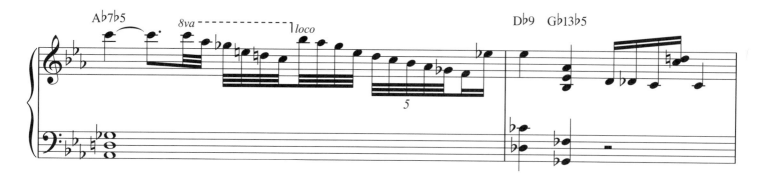

Ending
With freedom

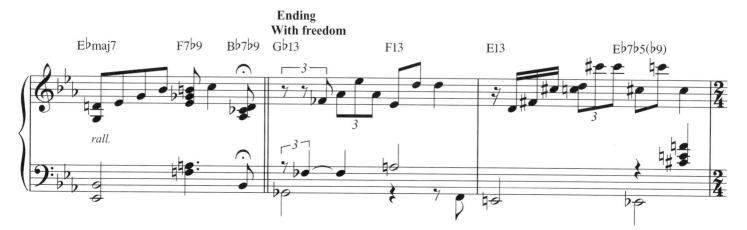

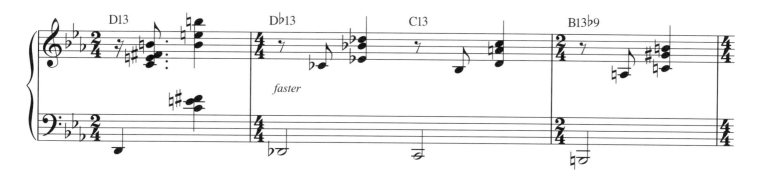

There's No One But You

from Barry Harris "Preminado"
Written by Redd Evans and Austen Croom-Johnson

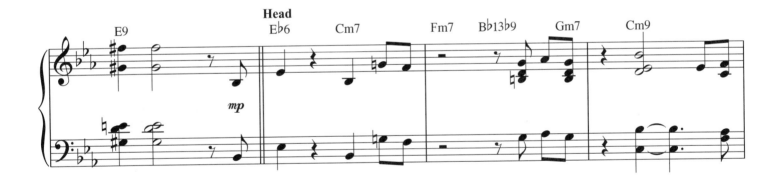

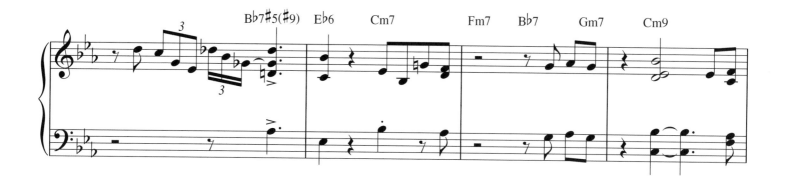

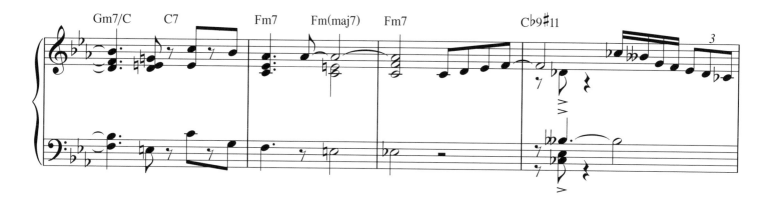

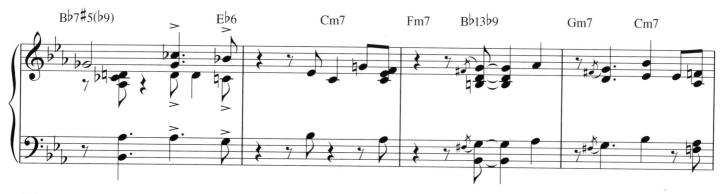

108

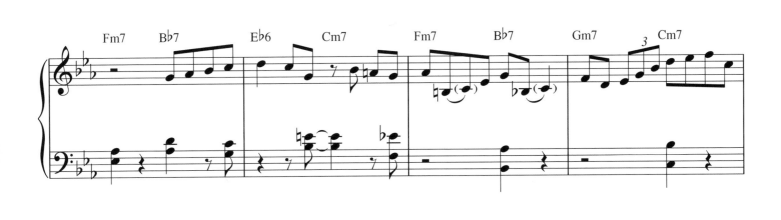

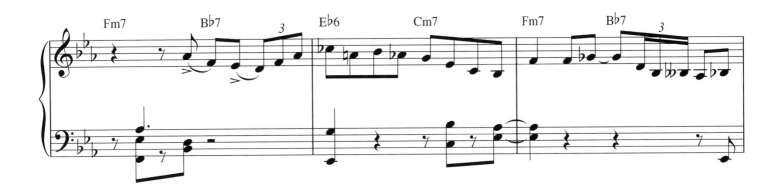

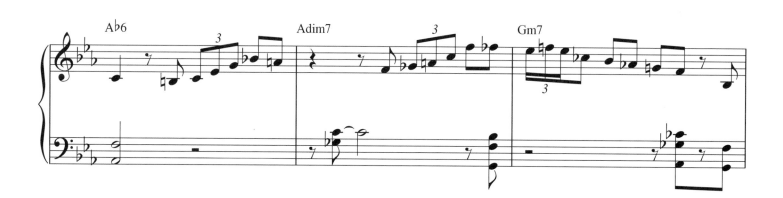

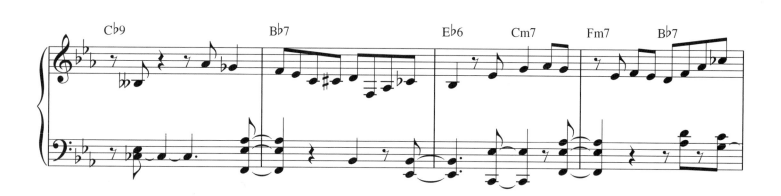

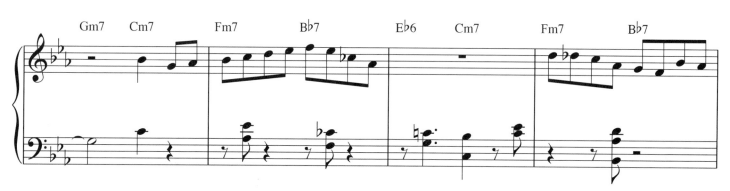

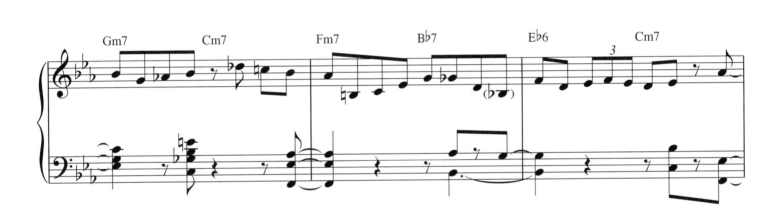

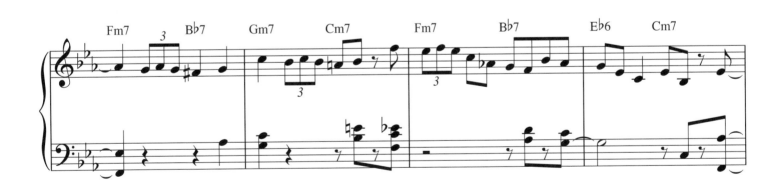

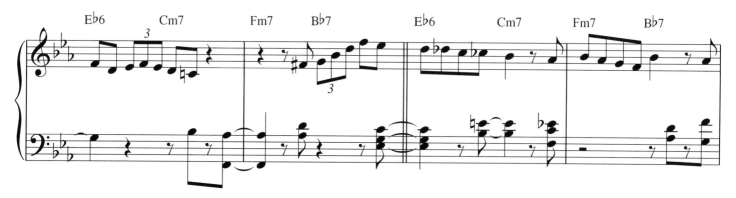

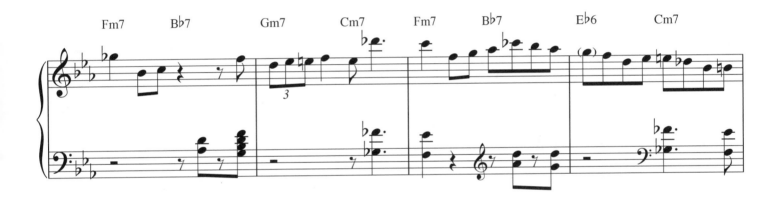

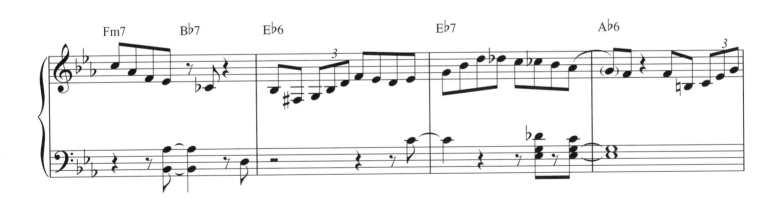

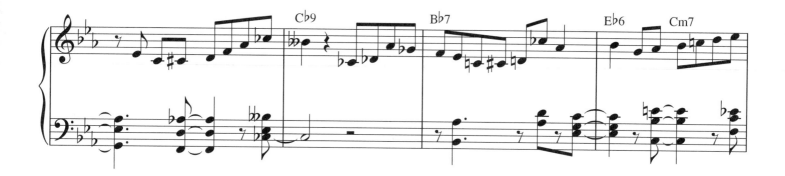

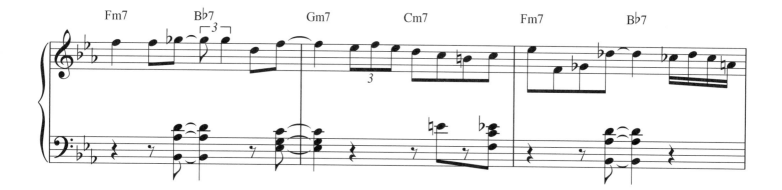

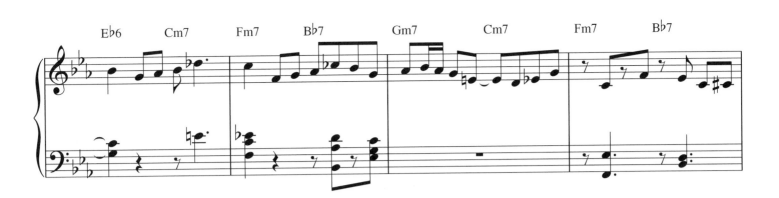

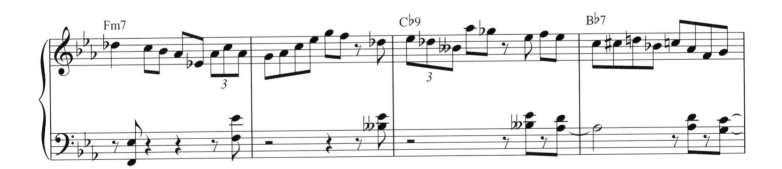

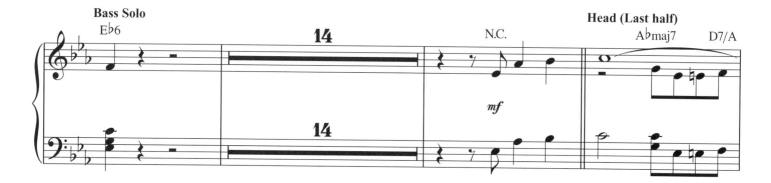

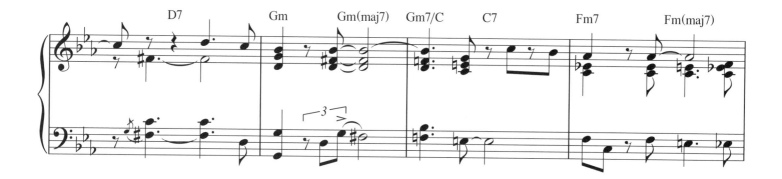

Ending

The Third World
from "The Prophetic Herbie Nichols, Vol 1"
By Herbie Nichols

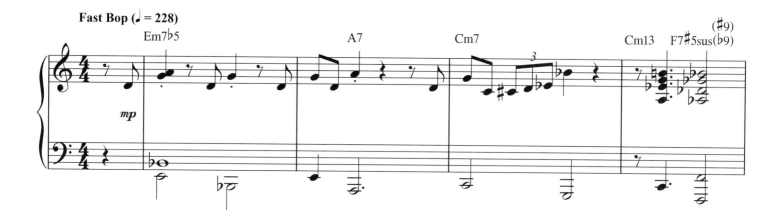

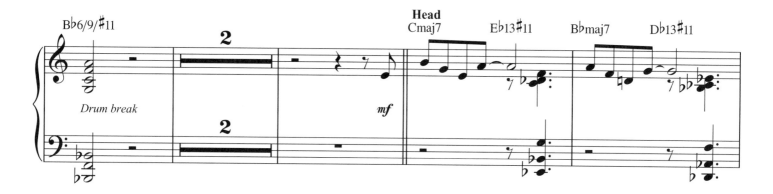

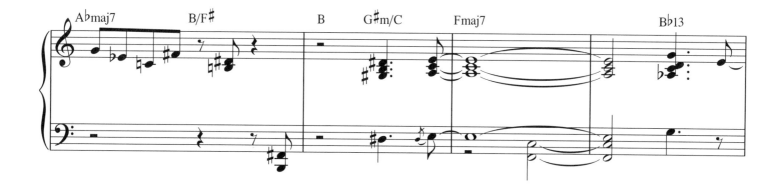

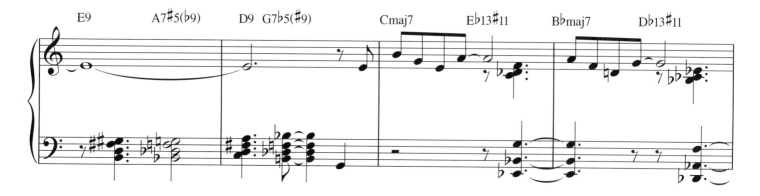

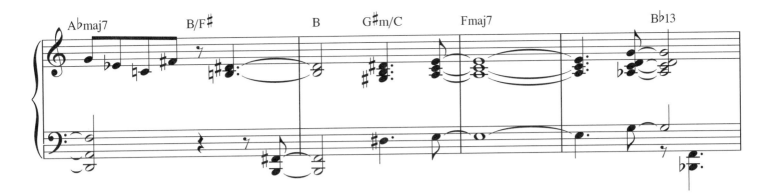

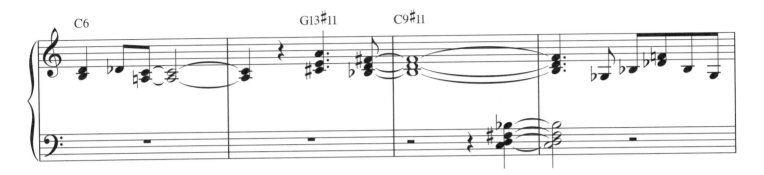

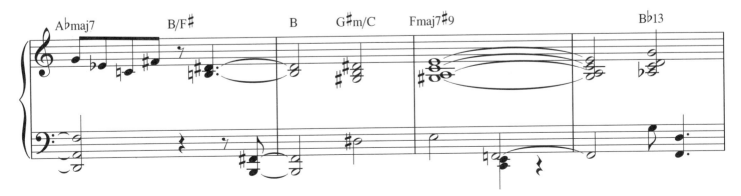

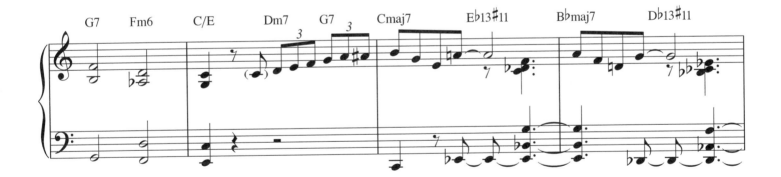

Piano Solo

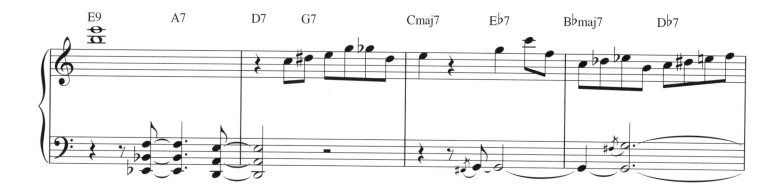

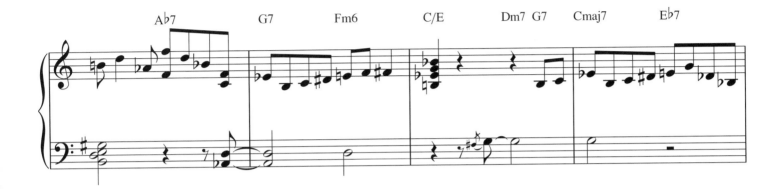

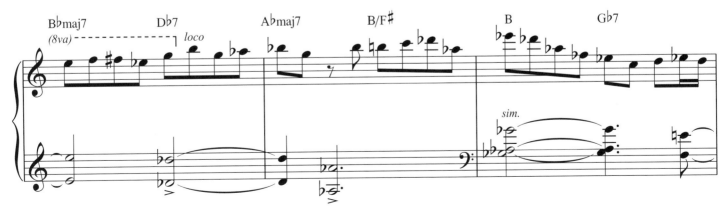

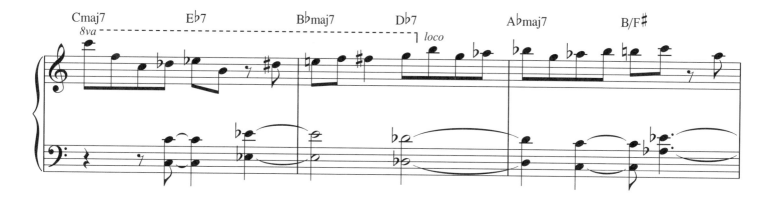

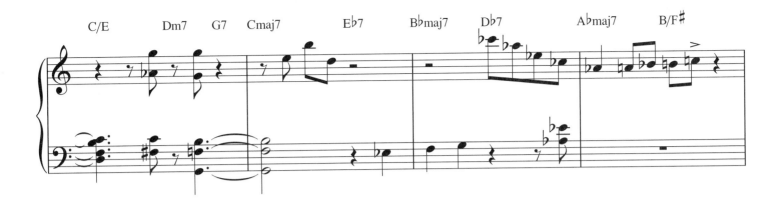

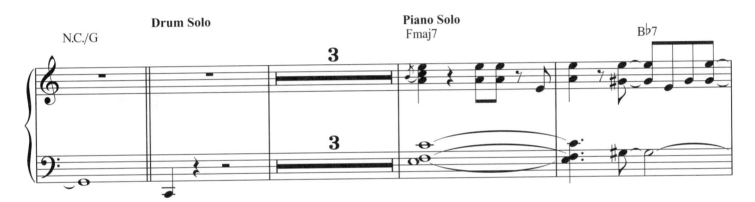

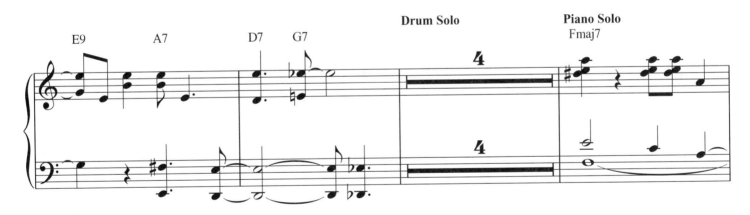

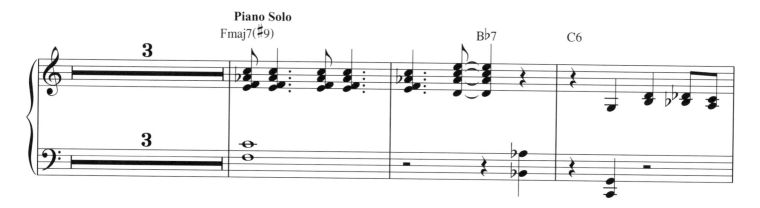

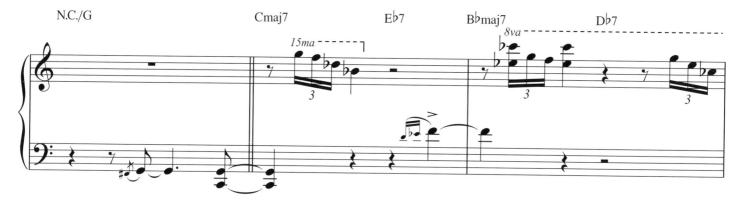

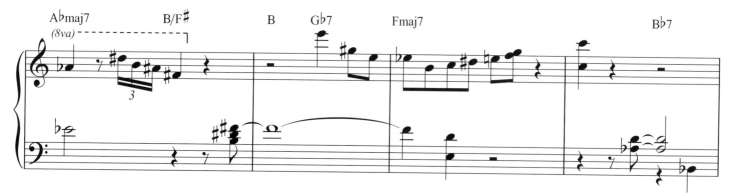

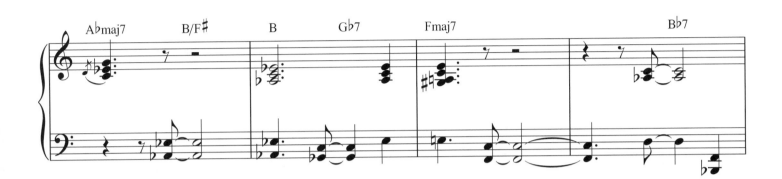

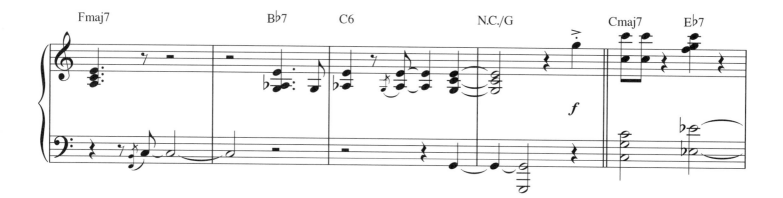

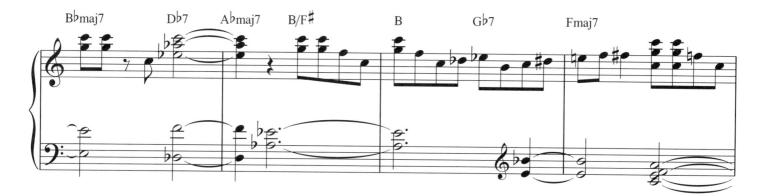

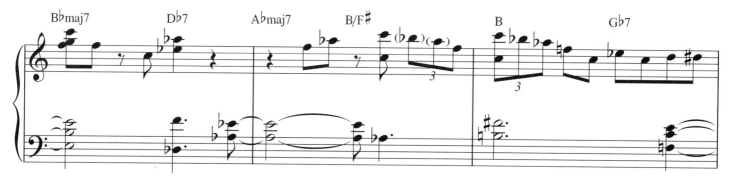

126

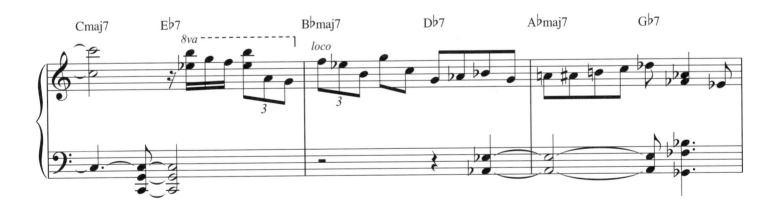

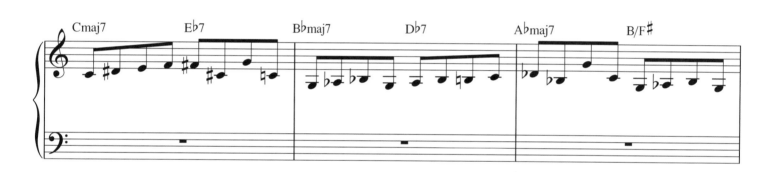

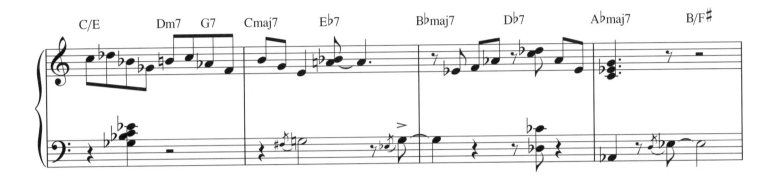

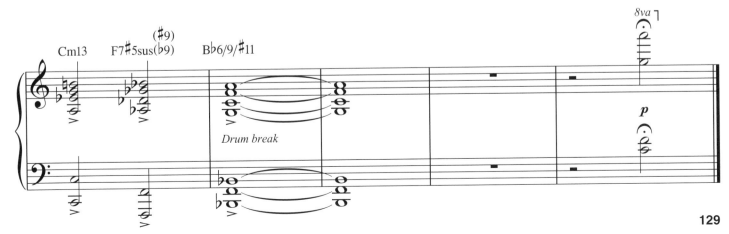

Un Poco Loco

from "The Amazing Bud Powell, Vol. 1"
By Earl "Bud" Powell

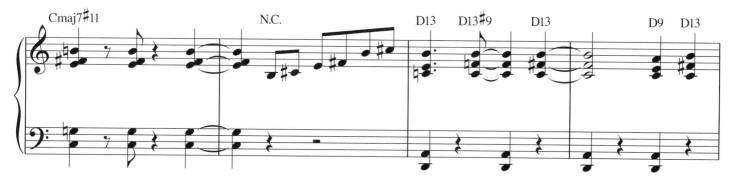

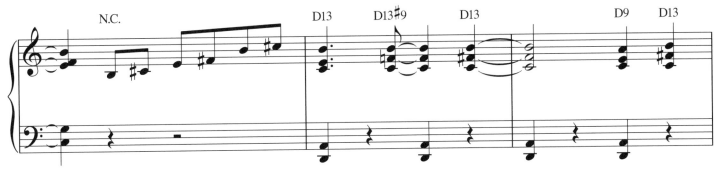

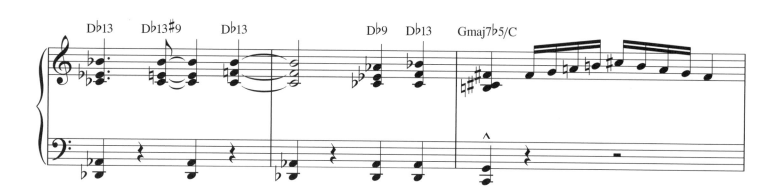

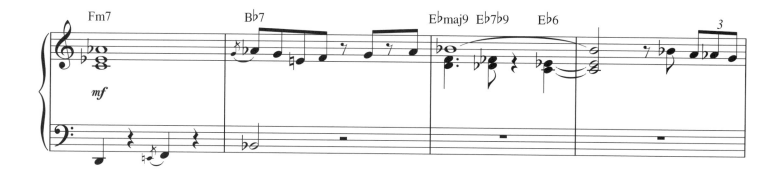

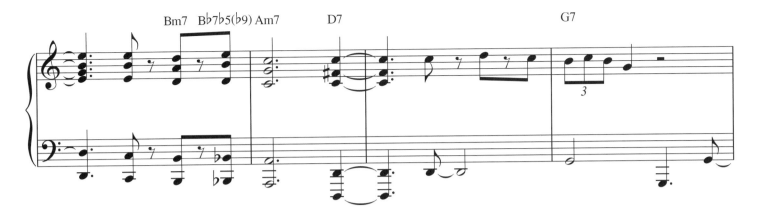

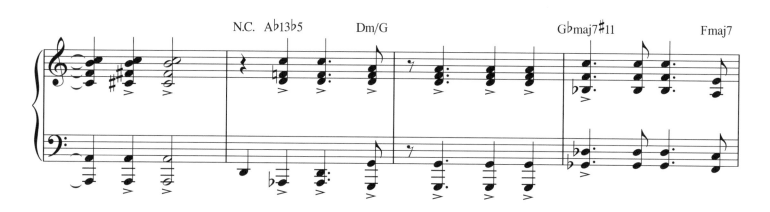

Piano Solo

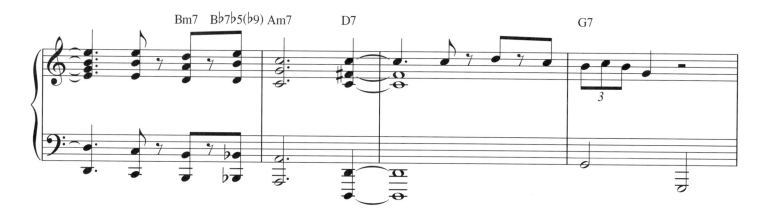

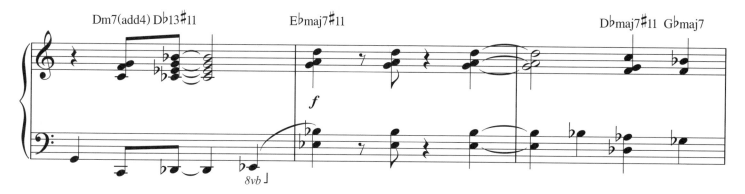

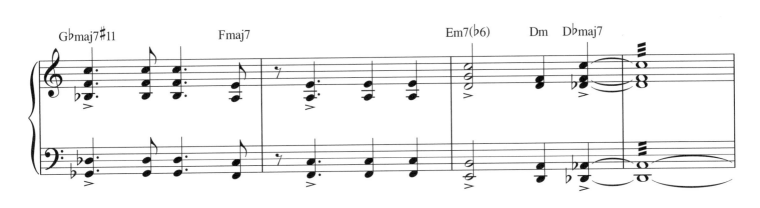

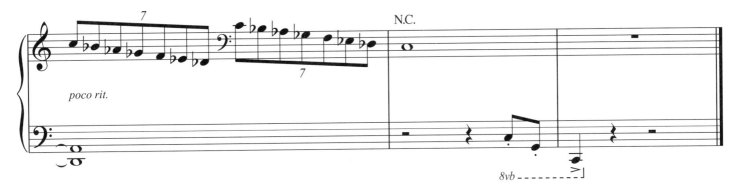

We're All Together

from Hank Jones "The Trio"
Words and Music by Hank Jones

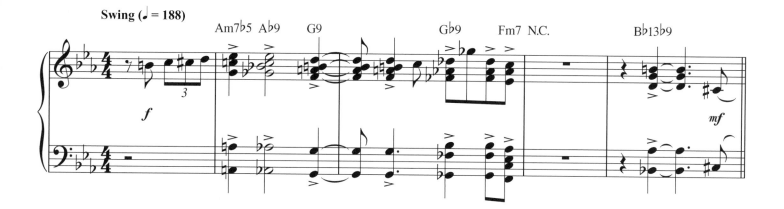

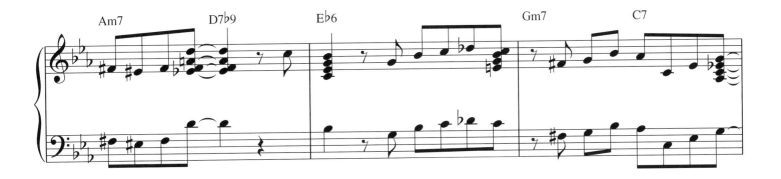

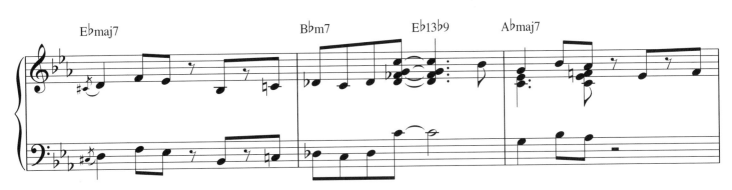

146

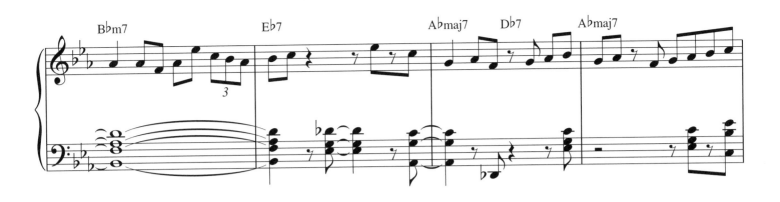

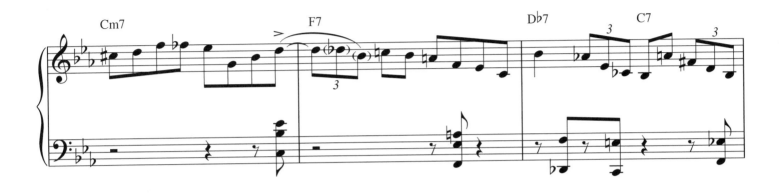

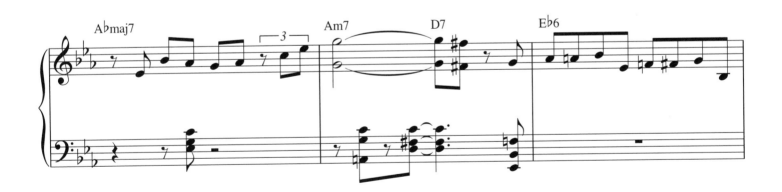

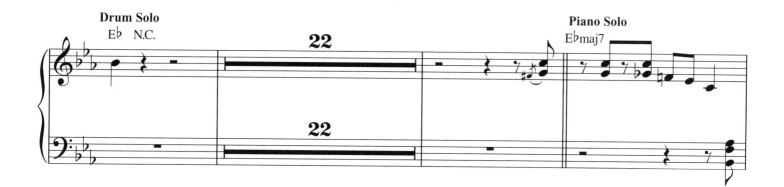

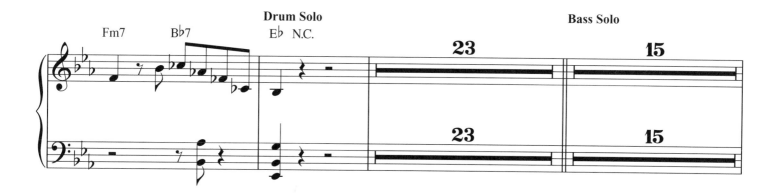

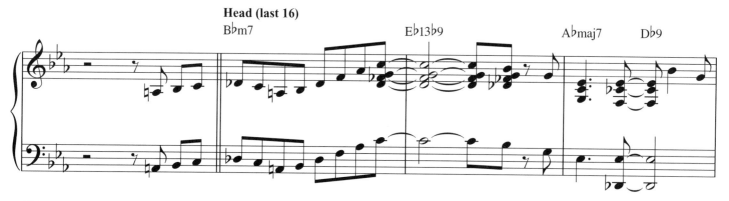

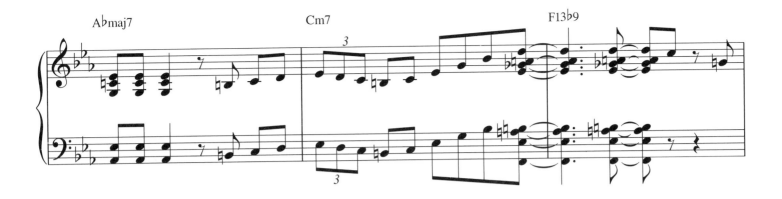

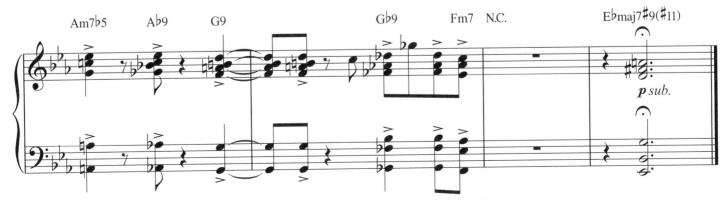

Whisper Not

from Wynton Kelly "Piano (Whisper Not)"
By Benny Golson

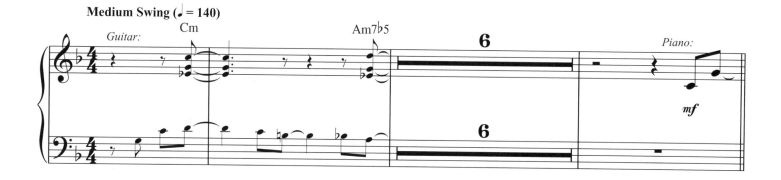

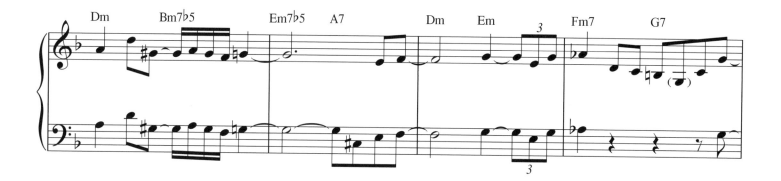

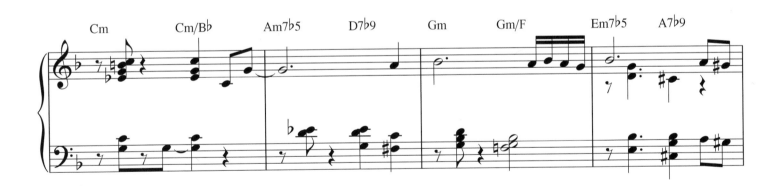

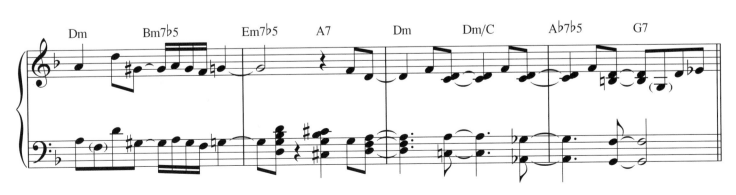

Piano Solo

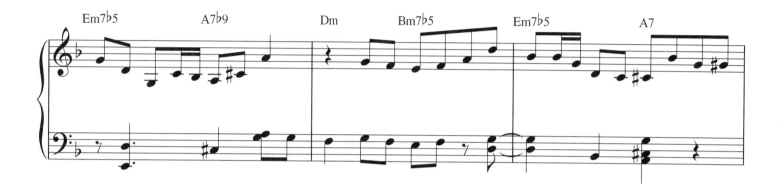

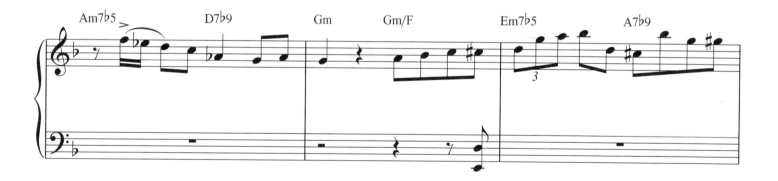

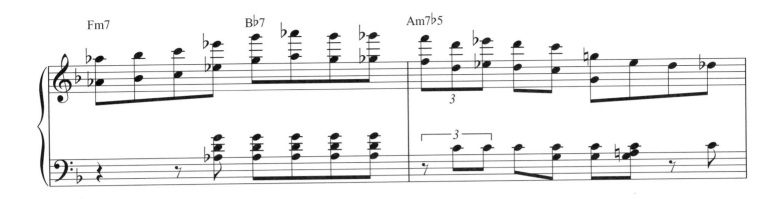

155

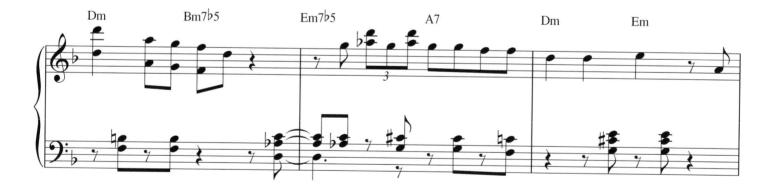

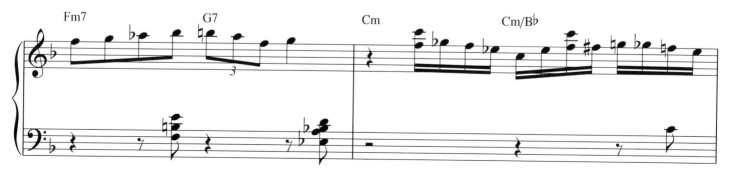

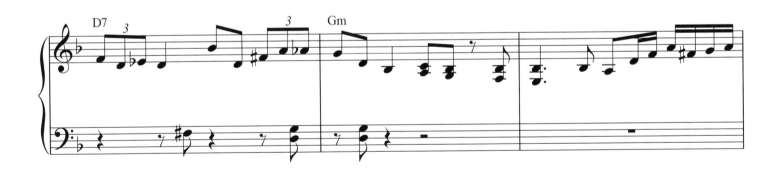

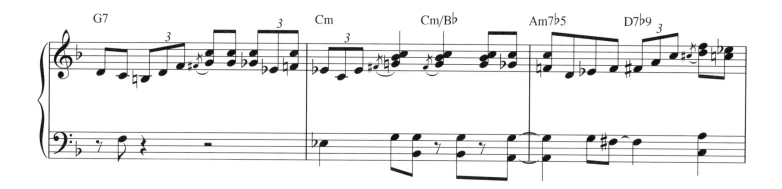

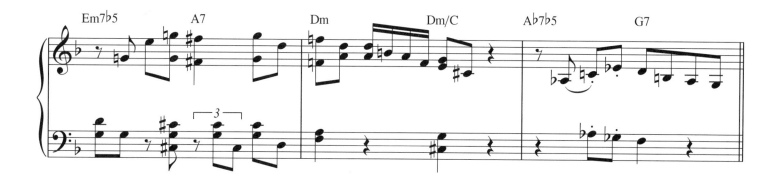

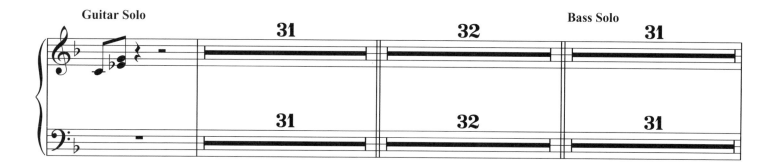

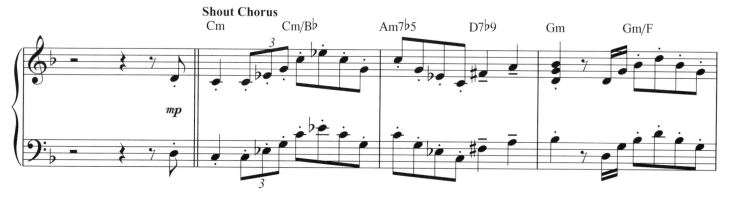

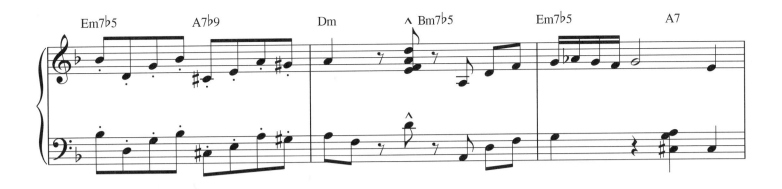

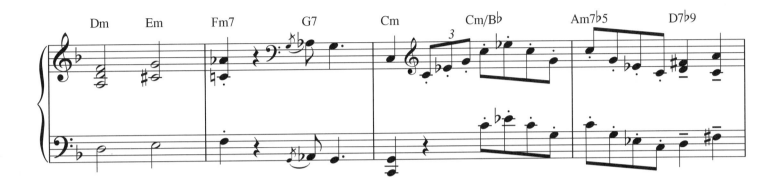

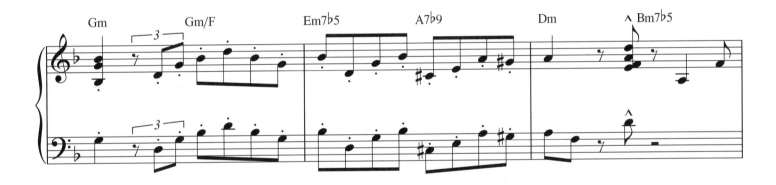

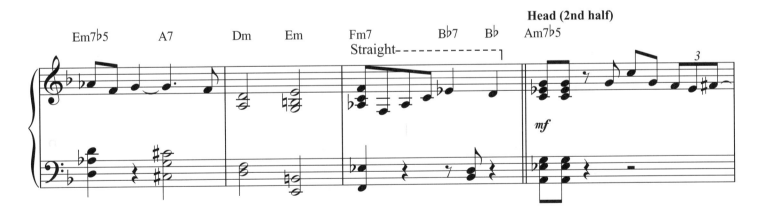

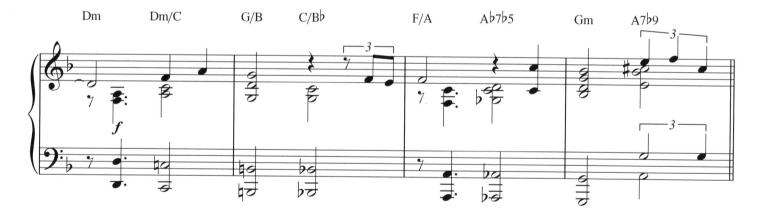

With freedom

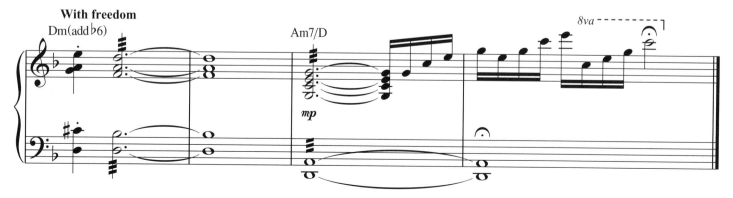